A
SHAPELY
FIRE

A SHAPELY FIRE

Changing the Literary Landscape

edited by Cyril Dabydeen

 **MOSAIC PRESS**
OAKVILLE NEW YORK LONDON

Canadian Cataloguing in Publication Data
Main entry under title:
A Shapely Fire : changing the literary landscape

ISBN 0-88962-345-7 (bound). – ISBN 0-88962-344-9 (pbk.)

1. Canadian literature (English) – Black authors. *
2. Canadian literature (English) – 20th century. *
I. Dabydeen, Cyril, 1945-

PS8235.B55S48 1987   C810'.8'0896   C87-094204-2
PR9194.5.B55S48 1987

Mosaic Press expresses its thank to the
Multiculturalism Directorate of the Department
of the Secretary of State for its generous support
of this publication. All the views expressed here,
however, are those of the authors alone.

Published by Mosaic Press, P.O. Box 1032,
Oakville, Ontario L6J 5E9 Canada. Office and
warehouse at 1252 Speers Rd., Unit 10,
Oakville, Ontario L6L 5N9 Canada.

Published with the assistance of the Canada
Council and the Ontario Arts Council.

MOSAIC PRESS:
In the United States:
Riverrun Press Inc., 1170 Broadway, Suite 807,
New York, N.Y., 10001, U.S.A.

In the U.K.:
John Calder (Publishers) Ltd., 18 Brewer
Street, London, W1R 4AS, England.

CONTENTS

ACKNOWLEDGEMENTS

It has been said that it would take a much longer time for an identifiable Caribbean-Canadian literature to evolve: longer, for instance, than it took Jewish-Canadian literature. However, I strongly believe that a fair amount of writing is being done in the closet which needed exposure. A study of the Caribbean authors' issue of *Tamarack Magazine* edited by William Toye, more than a decade ago, the book-length *Canada in Us Now* (NC Press, 1976), and the more recent emigré writing issue of *Prism International* (July 1984) inspired me to continue with this project towards a more focused approach. At the time of putting this together a second Black literature anthology, *Other Voices*, edited by Lorris Elliot (Williams-Wallace, 1986), and another small magazine issue of Caribbean writing via the *Toronto South Asian Review*, edited by Frank Birbalsingh, have appeared. I have been in touch with the editors of these in the sharing and gathering. In this context I wish to thank the Multiculturalism Directorate, Department of Secretary of State, for its support. I also wish to thank Seymour Mayne, Department of English, University of Ottawa, for his encouragement and advice; and, Howard Aster, for believing in this project.

The title is derived from a poem by A.J. Seymour. For other particulars of this book I wish to thank all the authors, most of whom directly submitted their work. For permission to publish or reproduce the material in this collection, grateful acknowledgement is made to the following:

LILLIAN ALLEN: for "Belly Woman's Lament" and "Marriage," first appeared in *Rhythm an' Hardtimes* (Toronto, Domestic Bliss, 1982), to the author. NEIL BISSOONDATH: for "Insecurity," from *Digging Up Mountains* (Macmillan and Co., 1985), to the publisher. DIONNE BRAND: for "P.P.S. Grenada," from *Chronicles of a Hostile Sun* (Williams-Wallace, 1984), to the author. DANIEL CAUDEIRON: for "Day Shift/Night Shift" (in *Ariel*), and "My Love is an African Woman," "Compulsion," and "Caribana: Toronto," to the author. AUSTIN CLARKE: for "Give it a Shot," from *When Women Rule* (McClelland and Stewart, 1985), to Jack McClelland and the author. MADELINE COOPSAMMY: for "The Tick-Tick Bicycle," to the author. CYRIL DABYDEEN: for "Rum-Running" (*Prism International*), "Sir James Douglas: Father of British Columbia" (*The Canadian Forum*), from *This Planet Earth* (Borealis Press, Ottawa, 1979), "Lenin Park," "My Country, North America, and the World," and "Ain't Got No Cash," to the author. MAX DORSINVILLE: for "Barbara," to the author. GERARD ETIENNE: for "Deaf Woman," to the author. HORACE GODDARD: for "Mamaetu" and "Conch Shell," to the author. KARL GORDON: for "Strangers at a Glance" and "Olympic Dream," to the author. CLAIRE HARRIS: for "Obatala" (*Arc*), "Blood Feud" (*Poetry Toronto*), and "Outposts," to the author. ABDUR-RAHMAN SLADE HOPKINSON: for "The Compass," "1968" and "Snowscape with Signature," to the author. ARNOLD ITWARU: for "The Faithful," from *Shattered Songs* (Aya Press, Toronto, 1983) and "ragblown roadless," to the author. ANTHONY PHELPS: for "The Father's Mouth," to the author. MARLENE PHILIP: for "Odetta," 'E. Pulcherrima," and "Salmon Courage," first appeared in *Salmon Courage* (Williams-Wallace, 1982), to the author. CHARLES ROACH: for "Poem, to Buddy Evans," to the author. SAM SELVON: for "Zeppi's Machine" (*Caribbean Studies* and CBC *Anthology*), to the author. RODERICK WALCOTT: for "Cul-de-Sac," to the author. EDWARD WATSON: for "Song My Lady Sings" (*Washington Review of the Arts*) and "Beyond the Reach of the Farthest Dream" (*Bim*, Barbados), to the author.

INTRODUCTION

The cultural life of the people from the Caribbean has always been many-sided and vibrant. I started this collection with that thought in mind as I reflected on the contributions of the various immigrant groups to Canadian society, one which over the years has moved well beyond the frontier image of a people who are essentially "drawers of water and hewers of wood" — to that of a nation primarily of urban dwellers with a sensibility accustomed to appreciating the admirable manifestations of the arts within its borders and abroad. While the cultural-cum-spiritual contributions of many of the immigrant groups have been documented, those of the people from the Caribbean, relatively speaking, have not. The reason for this is that the significant wave of immigrants from the Caribbean started arriving only recently, in the sixties and seventies, with the majority of the new immigrants being identifiably different from the mainstream. For these latter-day newcomers, the frontier took a different meaning: like their Europeans counterparts of an earlier period, they too were "drawers of water and hewers of wood," roughing it as domestic servants, factory and farm workers, security guards, railway conductors, and more recently as teachers and doctors — all the while expressing a vitality of spirit stemming from the active imagination that is the birthright of all.

The polyglot Caribbean peoples — whether they come from Jamaica, Trinidad, Barbados, Guyana, or Haiti — with a checkered history brought about primarily by the European ancestors of those who currently comprise the Canadian mainstream (in some instances these ancestors were the kin of the first settlers) have demonstrated a marked vitality despite the change in climate and geography, and even of the social system, that they encountered upon arriving here.

A Shapely Fire, in a sense, brings together in one collection a sample of that vitality in prose and poetry by Caribbean authors who have made their home in Canada. Writing, of course, is a significant part of Caribbean heritage; since the 1950s the region's authors have steadily been making a name for themselves in the United Kingdom and elsewhere; the imaginative vigour has since grown by leaps and bounds, and authors like the Naipauls, Derek Walcott, and E.R. Braithwaite are now respected world-wide. In Canada, a significant manifestation of that imaginative pulse is at work, continually shaping and being shaped by the spirit of the place, and undoubtedly, I believe, acting in such a way as to influence a re-definition of the conventional understanding of nationhood: from one viewed solely in terms of physical place to that which I have elsewhere referred to as based on a concept associated with the landscape of the mind, wherein place and psyche become intertwined in nation-building terms through the creative outpouring and meshing of the spirit. In this context, a real shaping is constantly taking place; the collective Canadian spirit is enhanced and enriched by the varied cultural streams and in the fusion of old and new traditions towards a vital celebration of the oneness of the evolving Canadian consciousness.

It can be said that, in Canada, the Caribbean literary groundwork has been laid in the seminal work of the Barbadian-born novelist Austin Clarke; his place in Canadian literature is well-established and needs no recounting. Around the time of the untimely death of Sonny Ladoo, another Trinidadian-born author (whose work is unfortunately not included in this collection), Sam Selvon, who had already built for himself a solid reputation while living in England, moved to Canada, and over the last few years has provided an added stimulation to the younger writers. With my own work starting to appear in the literary magazines in Canada in the seventies as I expressed the residues of sugar-plantation experiences in my Canadian beginnings, I watched with keen interest other poets, short story writers, and dramatists also appearing on the scene, some through the small (and large) publishing houses, as well as on the reading circuit. Of these new writers many are now becoming familiar to followers of developments of new streams in Canadian literature. Names like Neil Bissoondath. Dionne Brand, Claire Harris, Lillian Allen and others, while seen in a sense as a younger generation, will continue to be heard, will make their presences felt in the shaping of a more dynamic and all-embracing Canadian literature.

It might be said that in Canada there is no significant old or new generation of Caribbean authors, but rather an evolving literature. Thus, in this collection, the reader will be able to observe, feel and identify with the variety expressed here. One will be likely to experience with all the writers the immediacy of beginnings — in what has been called the *there*, the place where one came from, seen in terms of the palpable residues of the spirit manifested in powerful feelings, often of nostalgia, or of seeking an enduring identity — coupled with the *here*, temperate Canada, where the Caribbean spirit asserts itself in the desire to forge a wholesome and meaningful existence, oftentimes in a spirit of quest and in the overall desire to find a shared meaning, a deeper significance, in life.

Some of the *there* can be seen in Sam Selvon's short story "Zeppi's Machine," reflecting the traditional society undergoing inevitable change; or, in Roderick Walcott's play "Cul-de-Sac," which explores the return to the eighteenth century, in a sense to update history and to re-orient the mind about an important facet of the pre-colonial period when the Caribbean was the battleground for the European powers. In some of the poetry, too, we see a significant return, this time to ancestral sources for its metaphorical energy, in Claire Harris, for instance, it is expressed in the form of a spiritual odyssey to Africa as the speaker fuses those experiences with the present; in Marlene Philip, virtually the same fusion but with a distinctive cadence holds true. In Neil Bissoondath's story, appropriately entitled "Insecurity," the attempts at bridging to the *here* but with undertones of violence and a dark fear also form part of the reality which could be seen, in a sense, as building upon the story, "The Tick Tick Bicycle," by Madeline Coopsammy.

In Austin Clarke's "Give it a Shot," interaction and conflict inevitably occur, registering the irony inherent in the *here*, or the life in Canada. In other stories and poems, too, the present reality becomes the focus for the quest towards a vibrant self-expression and fulfillment. Whether observed in Max Dorsinville's reflection on overseas yearnings from a Haitian perspective, or in Gerard Etienne's depictions of voodoo impulses at work in Montreal, or even in Daniel Caudeiron's fusion of urban mythology with current personal motifs, the same themes and feelings virtually exist. In Anthony Phelps, both *here* and *there* are finally welded into a mythopoeic paean distinctively African and Caribbean and extending to the universal through the energy of sheer texture.

Inevitably there is a demotic, creolese and *dub* strain in the poetry, which is integral with the general cadence and lilt of West Indian speech rhythms and vernacular forms seen *par excellence* in the writings of Louise Bennet. Sometimes this tradition is manifested in the tense fusion of celebration and protest, as seen in the poetry of Lillian Allen, Charles Roach, and Horace Goddard, where the renditions may embrace colourful and even racy expressions, giving the work its unique resonance and power. Counterpointed with this form of "orality" are the more individualistic perspectives of protest in the depiction of ideology as manifested in poignant images associated with invasion, as seen in Dionne Brand's poetry; in Arnold Itwaru's, the individual psyche takes on aspects of the wounded consciousness in the portrayal of states of decay and disorientation without the need to delineate physical boundaries associated with "eelgrass and snow." Clearly, the Caribbean heritage is not depicted in terms of fun and frolic or exemplified in vapid images of the "faery isles."

Altogether, the poetry and prose illuminate the wide range of the human spirit in the desire to share common truths and to express personal visions within those of a wider world. In arranging this collection the desire has been to portray this facet as well as to reflect a measure of particularity of the diverse islands, with only the barest inkling to limit the writers in terms of specific subject matter or mode. Thus, the poetry of Abdur-Rahman Slade Hopkinson, Edward Watson, and Karl Gordon attest to this even as they maintain their individual pungency. For this reason, too, most of the works collected

11

here are in English, even though a sample of the Haitian temperament is presented (in translation) in order to expose the reader to as wide a view as possible of the Caribbean psyche; in this context I apologize to those writers who might also have easily been included in this collection but for lack of space or other considerations beyond my control.

It is hoped that the individual works as a whole will portray their own aesthetic in the light of the originality of perception of each author. At the same time it is also hoped that this literature will make its collective impact of the Caribbean presence in Canada more strongly felt and perhaps engender a greater flow of the well-spring of the creative imagination from our Caribbean-born writers towards a lasting Canadian art and life.

Cyril Dabydeen
June 1986

A NOTE ON THE CONTRIBUTORS

LILLIAN ALLEN
Born in Jamaica, she worked for a while as a domestic in Toronto soon after arriving in Canada. She graduated from York University and is currently a grass roots activist and feminist. She is a member of the Toronto group, *de dub* poets, and has published two chapbooks via Domestic Bliss, a cooperative enterprise in Toronto. She has read widely from her work in Canada; she recently won a Juno Award.

NEIL BISSOONDATH
Born in Trinidad in 1955, he immigrated to Toronto in 1973 to attend York University where he graduated with a degree in French. A nephew of V.S. Naipaul, he has published a highly-praised first collection of stories, *Digging Up Mountains* (Macmillan, Toronto, 1985). He currently teaches in a private school in Toronto and is working on a novel.

DIONNE BRAND
Originally from Trinidad, Dionne Brand has been living in Canada since 1970. Educated at York University and the Ontario Institute for Studies in Education, she is an activist in the immigrant community. She has published four books of poetry, the latest of which is *Chronicles of a Hostile Sun* (Williams-Wallace, 1984). She was present in Grenada during the American invasion of the island in 1984. She makes her home in Toronto.

DANIEL CAUDEIRON
Born in Venezuela on July 26, 1942 of British and French West Indian parents, he was educated in Trinidad, Dominica, and Britain, where he lived for a number of years before immigrating to Canada in 1974. He is actively involved in theatre, Caribbean music, and television. He has been anthologized in *Carifesta: New Writing* (1981). His own poetry collections are *Poems* (1973) and *Cheers and Jeers* (1982). He lives in Toronto.

AUSTIN CLARKE
Perhaps the best-known of the Caribbean writers in Canada, Clarke was born in Barbados. He attended the University of Toronto and later did an assortment of jobs, including documentary work for the CBC, taught in numerous American universities, and served as Cultural Attaché to the Barbados Embassy in Washington, D.C. Among his many novels are *The Prime Minister* and *Growing Up Stupid Under*

the Union Jack. His latest book is *Nine Men Who Laughed* (Penguin Books, 1986).

MADELINE COOPSAMMY

Born in Trinidad in 1939, she attended St. Joseph's Convent in Port-of-Spain, the University of Delhi, and the University of Manitoba. Her short spell in India was the result of an attempt to find her roots long before it was fashionable to do so. She is married with two children. At present she is a homemaker and writer in Portage lá Prairie, Manitoba where, with her family, she is "part of the scenery."

CYRIL DABYDEEN

A Guyanese by birth, he came to Canada in 1970. He finished his formal education at Queen's University with an M.A. degree (English) and a Master of Public Administration degree, and has since published in most of the Canadian literary magazines. His work has been anthologized in Canada, Denmark, the U.S., Britain, and New Zealand. He has written six books of prose and poetry, his latest being *Islands Lovelier than a Vision* (Peepal Tree Press, Leeds, Britain). He was the Poet Laureate of Ottawa from 1984 to 1987, and currently lives in that city.

MAX DORSINVILLE

A reputable scholar on the Caribbean, Max Dorsinville originally hailed from Haiti and currently teaches in the Department of English, McGill University, in Montreal. He has travelled widely. His works have appeared in numerous journals in Canada and the U.S. His *Caliban Without Prospero: Essays on Quebec and Black Literature* was published in 1974.

GERARD ETIENNE

Gerard Etienne originally came to Canada from Haiti. A well-known poet and novelist, he teaches in the French Department at the Université de Moncton, New Brunswick. His latest novel is *Une Femme Muette*, an excerpt of which is included in this collection in English; the book-length translation is scheduled to appear soon.

HORACE GODDARD

Born in Barbados in 1947, he came to Canada in 1970. He holds degrees from Concordia, McGill, and Montreal universities, graduating from the latter with a Ph.D. in English. He has published a volume of poems, *Rastaman: Poems for Leonta* as well as a one-act play, *Rainbow Country*. He says, "I am trying to work on some short stories in Barbadian dialect and I am compiling a book of Barbadian proverbs with the view of tracing their origin and currency in the West Indian folk tradition."

KARL GORDON

Jamaican-born, he was educated at the University of the West Indies, and later did post-graduate work in Linguistics in Canada. Currently

14

a high school teacher in Ottawa, he is also active in Third World Players, of which he is a driving force. He has done public performances of his work on stage and on TV.

CLAIRE HARRIS

She came to Canada in 1966 from her native Trinidad. Currently living Calgary, she is a school teacher and photographer. She has widely published poetry in the small magazines in Canada, and is a poetry editor of *Dandelion*. Two books of her poetry have recently appeared via Fiddlehead Press and Williams-Wallace Publications.

ABDUR-RAHMAN SLADE HOPKINSON

He was born in Guyana in 1934, educated there and at the University of the West Indies, where he was active in theatre as both actor and director. He studied at the Yale Drama School and later founded the Caribbean Theatre Guild. He came to Canada in 1977, and is currently active as a journalist with Toronto's *Share* newspaper. His books of poetry are *The Four and Other Poems*, *The Madwoman of Papine*, and *The Friend*. He makes his home in Toronto.

ARNOLD ITWARU

Born in 1942, he came to Canada in 1969 and attended the University of Toronto and York University. A sociologist, he has published poetry and short stories in *Nebula* and *Quarry*. A book of poetry, *Shattered Songs* (Aya Press), appeared in 1982. He currently teaches at York University in Toronto.

ANTHONY PHELPS

He was born in Haiti in 1928 and has worked as a journalist for Radio Canada. Phelps has published a dozen books of poetry and has won the Casa de lás Americas Literary Prize (Cuba). His work has been translated into English, Spanish, Russian, Bulgarian, and German. He alternates between Montreal and Mexico at the present.

MARLENE PHILIP

Trinidadian-born, Marlene Nourbese Philip is a writer/lawyer who has lived in Canada since 1968. She has published two books, *Thorns* and *Salmon Courage* (Williams-Wallace). In 1983 she was awarded a Canada Council grant to prepare a taped documentary, "Blood is for Bleeding" (The Positive Values of the Menstrual Experience). "My work attempts a fusion of the disparate threads that make up the new world experience," she writes.

CHARLES ROACH

Trinidadian by birth, he is an activist civil rights lawyer in Toronto. His previous work is *Roots for the Ravens*. He has also published broadsheets of his poems and has done public readings of his work in Toronto and elsewhere under the sponsorship of the Canada Council.

SAM SELVON

Well-known Trinidadian novelist and short story writer, Sam Selvon has written over a dozen books while living in Britain during the period from 1950 to 1978. He has received many awards for his writing in Britain, the U.S. and the Caribbean. His latest book is *Moses Ascending*. He is currently at work on his autobiography. His more recent appearances have been as Visiting Assistant Professor, University of Victoria; Visiting Instructor, Banff School of Fine Arts' and Creative Writer in the International Program at the University of Iowa. He now resides in Calgary where he is Writer-in-Residence at the university.

RODERICK WALCOTT

A St. Lucian, he was born together with poet Derek Walcott on January 23, 1930. He was drama leader of the St. Lucia Arts Guild from 1951 to 1968, a group formed by his brother. After 1968 he attended York University to study Fine Arts. He has received the Order of the British Empire, and has written numerous plays and has appeared in many Caribbean anthologies. He now lives in Montreal with his family.

EDWARD WATSON

Originally from Jamaica, he currently teaches English at the University of Windsor, Ontario. He has published a wide range of articles, and his poetry has appeared in a number of small magazines. A volume of poems, *Out of the Silent Stone* (Bruckings Publishing House), appeared in 1976. His forthcoming work is *Epitaphs Where Journeys End*.

PROSE

ZEPPI'S MACHINE

SAM SELVON

Zeppi sat on the wooden steps in front of his thatched hut early in the morning watching the sun creep over the tip of the green hills and spread light on the small village sprawled in the valley below him, and move on to throw a warm glow of gold on the rolling canefields. In a few minutes that pleasant warmth would become uncomfortable, then hot, and apart from a scudding cloud or two the day would settle down to a steel-blue sky and the labourers in the fields would be drenched in perspiration. By and by Zeppi would see Meena come out to milk the cow in the yard: he had given her a concoction for her husband Jaldo, who had a bad cough. Rosa, Meena's neighbour, would come out to broadcast grains of left-over boiled rice for her fowls, and chat with Meena for a while. Felix, her husband, would still be sleeping after a night of gambling. It was probable he never ate breakfast, for many mornings Zeppi had seen him come dashing out with his shirt in his hands and hurry off to the canefields. Rosa wanted Zeppi to work an obeah on Felix so he would stop gambling. On the other hand Felix wanted a lucky charm so he would always win.

Zeppi saw smoke coming from the kitchen shed behind Lutchman's shop. The old East Indian, mixed with a little Chinese blood, never came to Zeppi with his problems, or to find out what the future had in store for him. Perhaps he was afraid, or skeptical, or a little of both. But Zeppi got free drinks and deferential treatment whenever he visited the shop. He had a stool near the bar, and if it was occupied it became vacant the moment he appeared.

Zeppi himself had reached a stage where he was not sure if he was gifted, or just plain lucky, or if he was a one-eye man in a blind-eye village. Years of preparing potions and lotions, of giving counsel to patch up broken relationships, of divining the weather and forecasting prosperity or ill-fortune, had engendered in him a belief that perhaps he did possess supernatural powers. The villagers in Tacarigua swore by him, and he would be a great fool to argue. Instead he backed their superstition and fear by surrounding himself with a vast array of every conceivable object identified with his art. His hut was cluttered with all the paraphernalia associated with an obeahman, from Zanteelay, an enormous *mapipire* snake free to roam, to a human skull hanging in the entrance. Surrounded by these things day and night, Zeppi had strange dreams which he puzzled over when day broke, sometimes wishing that he was the suppliant and not the interpreter of dreams and phantasies.

He hoped that today somebody would turn up with cash. He had two baskets overflowing with tomatoes — before payday the villagers brought whatever they could. When Meena appeared with a bulging paper bag he was sure it was tomatoes; there was a glut in the village.

"You people think tomatoes is all I live on?" he scowled. "Even Zanteelay tired eating it." He tossed one and it burst open on the snake's head in the corner; muscle rippled as Zanteelay coiled up and looked at Meena, who backed away.

"You come for more medicine for Jaldo, eh?"

"Yes Zeppi." She did not ask him how he knew. "Make it stronger this time, he still coughing and can't go to work."

"You didn't give him the first dose exactly at midday like I told you?"

"We don't have no clock to tell midday."

"Well, then." He began to prepare the medicine.

"Lutchman putting two new machines in the shop, Zeppi, to make more business."

"Machines is trouble in Tacarigua. You self remember when they bring that harvester machine in the fields, how it take away work from the labourers."

"Yes, but these is a different kind. One is a jukebox to play music, and the other one could tell your weight and fortune."

"That's a lot of nonsense, Meena. You think a machine better than a man brains?"

"I don't know, but it look like machine-invasion in Tacarigua, because tomorrow the government sending a mobile x-ray unit to take out photos of everybody, to make sure they don't have T.B."

Zeppi laughed. He was a big man and it was more of a rumbling deep in his chest, and it came out hollow.

"It's no joke," Meena said. "All the workers getting time off to attend. You think if they take out Jaldo photo he will get better?"

"This *vetee-vay* and *demee-semee* mixture should fix him up." Zeppi shook the bottle vigorously as he handed her. "And don't come back here with no rotten tomatoes. Money does make my powers work best. Unless you want to buy a camera for me to take photos too!"

His laughter rolled after her as she went down the hill. But he grew a little thoughtful, thinking about the machine-invasion.

The big event in Tacarigua was payday, but it was as nothing compared to the excitement when the x-ray unit parked in front of the shop, and Lutchman played his jukebox loud to attract a crowd. Even the children loitered on their way to school in the next village.

Meena and Jaldo were in animated conversations with Rosa and Felix, who had both been inside the van already.

"It's not your face they take out," Rosa was saying, "it's inside your body."

"But what you have to do when you go in there?" Meena asked.

"Well, they take down your name, then you have to strip naked as you born..."

"Big lie!" Felix interrupted. "You only trying to frighten poor Meena. It's only my shirt I had to take off."

"Don't listen to Felix, child. Hear me. Then you stand up in front of this machine, and put your hands on your waist." Rosa pantomimed the movement.

"What for?" Jaldo demanded. "Is dancing or what?"

"Maybe it make the picture come out better. Anyway, you got to stand still. And when I say still, I mean *still*, not *one* move. You take a de-eep breath, and hold it. Like this. Watch."

"You forget a part," Felix said. "You forget the part when you have to rest your chin on top the machine, to help you keep still."

Rosa could not answer because her lungs were filled with air and she was holding the pose for all to see. Her eyes were bulging and her cheeks puffed out before she blew out. "Then the machine go whir-rr, and it finish."

"You mean they don't give you no injection and operate on you?" Jaldo asked.

"Go and see for yourself — it's your turn now," Rosa said.

Meena gave him a push to hurry him up — the crowd was restless and the sun was hot, they wanted to get it over with and go into the shop for a cool drink and to try out the machines. Rosa and Felix went in, telling Meena to meet them there when Jaldo was through.

There was no shade except that cast by the unit itself, and that spot was already occupied. Meena, roasting in the open, was thinking of joining Rosa when she saw Zeppi approaching. as he came up some-one shouted: "Aye Zeppi! You come to take your photo too?"

Another answered for the obeahman: "The great Zeppi don't need no x-ray like we, man. He deal with spirits and powers!"

"Tell them, tell them," Zeppi said, "tell them they only wasting time here in the hot sun. You-all letting some stupid machine fool you?"

"The *government* send it," a woman said, and a chorus of voices agreed, as if the government was some immense and mysterious power that controlled and manipulated their lives from a distance, and they were helpless to do anything about it. But it was the accept-ance of fatalism too, and the shirking of responsibility: whatsoever the outcome, praise the lord it would rest on the government's head.

"Who get you better when you sick?" Zeppi growled. "Who bring rain when the river dry? Who solve all your troubles when you in dis-tress and got no one to turn to? Not no blasted government!" He looked scornfully at them. "You people must be crazy to stand up here in the hot sun thinking that machine could do anything for you."

Just then Jaldo came out of the unit. Spotting him Zeppi gestured and said: "Look at Jaldo, just one dose of my medicine and he be able to walk about from his sickbed."

21

"Zeppi," Jaldo said, "that woman in there tell me some stupidness that I got a shadow on my lungs!"

"You hear that?" Zeppi made his big laugh. "Come over her, Jaldo come." He swung his arms to make a circle of space in the crowd. "Come and stand up right here."

Jaldo moved into the circle.

"All right. Look down there on the ground in front of you, and tell me what it is you see there?"

"My shadow!" Jaldo was relieved.

"It looks like you, don't it? It belongs to you. If you anywhere, it follow you. Everybody got shadows, man Look at mines. And yours, and yours," he pointed in the crowd, and everyone began to shuffle and look for their shadows.

The reflections moved into each other, forming irregular patterns as the head and shoulders of one merged into another, or legs and arms became distorted and confused: it was as if a scene reflected in a calm pond had been shattered by a stone. It almost came to a brawl as they pushed and shoved for a piece of land to cast their shadows upon and make indentifying movements.

"I live with shadows all the time," Zeppi said, and turned to go into the shop. Most of the crowd followed him, but Meena held Jaldo back.

"You sure she say 'shadow'? Maybe she say 'parasite' or 'germ' and you didn't hear?" She was concerned for him.

Jaldo coughed and shot the phlegm from his throat a good twelve feet away. "I hear what I hear. Let's get out this hot sun, man."

Lutchman was behind the counter, rubbing his hands as if he were caressing the dollars he anticipated this unusual morning. The arrival of the unit had coincided with the installation of the machines, and this was his first free moment from attending to the horde of customers. Felix and three other men were gambling in a corner with a new pack of cards that cost a dollar, and the d rinks on their table was worth another five. The jukebox and weighing machine were eating up coins as fast as the excited villagers could put them in. Only Zeppi sat alone on his stool, scowling and brooding at all the attention centered on the machines.

Rosa told Meena, "You just have to put your money in the slot, girl, and the music will come out. Wait till this record finish and I will show you."

"What about this one?" Meena moved to it.

"That tell your weight and fortune. Just wait till we get a chance and I will work it."

A minute later Rosa made Meena step up on the base and put in a coin.

"One hundred and ten pounds," the machine said.

"What you say?" Meena asked it.

22

Rosa burst out laughing. "It can't talk to you, only your weight. See what your fortune is."

Meena took the little card that came out and read aloud: "Great prosperity is in store. Don't believe everything you hear."

"Ain't it amazing?" Rosa said. "We don't need Zeppi no more to tell the future!"

Zeppi heard his name above the noise, and called: "What's that you saying about me, Rosa?"

"I say this machine like it have more powers than you!"

As she spoke the jukebox stopped and they all heard. A hush fell as Zeppi strode to the machine.

"Oh?" He towered over Rosa. "You best watch your mouth, Rosa, before your teeth fall out!"

Rosa put her hand to her mouth and muttered something.

"I don't need no machine to tell what you weigh," Zeppi said. "A skinny little piece of cane like you don't weigh more than ninety pounds for the most!"

Rosa stepped on the machine and put a coin in.

"One hundred and twenty pounds." This time the machine intoned the words like Zeppi himself when he was casting a spell.

"A-agh!" Before he could control himself his bare foot lashed out and he kicked the machine. Simultaneously with a howl of pain he was glaring around to see if anyone dared to laugh.

"You-all best hads watch watch your step! You-all best hads respect my powers before I stop the rain from falling and cause a drought in Tacarigua!"

Rain fell that instant, with the suddenness that sometimes happens in the tropics. A passing cloud, heavy with moisture, burst over the village and rain pattered and pinged on the galvanised roof of the shop. in a few minutes it would clear up and the sun would be blazing again as if it never happened.

Emboldened by the omen, Meena tittered. Rosa giggled. Jaldo chuckled, and by the time Felix guffawed everyone was making his or her variation on laughter, and the rain-water gurgled in the spout on the roof.

It was a bad moment for Zeppi. Shaking his head and muttering imprecations, he stormed out of the shop.

The week that followed gave Zeppi a lot of time to brood and ponder over his diminishing authority in the village. Business was slack, the only one who came to consult him was an old labourer, whose eyesight was failing naturally, anyway. Zeppi gave him a stick to go about with — "this stick is your eye" — and threw the old man's tomatoes out of the window.

It was this last action — while doing it — that he thought about pitching everything out of his hut and modernising his trade to keep up with the times in Tacarigua. The very day he made up his mind,

23

and took a trip to Port-of-Spain, getting a lift from a van driver who came to deliver goods to the shop.

Two days later Meena came, worried about Jaldo's illness. She stood in the entrance completely stunned by what she saw. Not a single vestige of the obeahman's accoutrements or trappings were to be seen, it was as if a wind had swept everything away, even Zanteelay had vanished. She hardly recognised Zeppi in a jazzy coloured shirt and a pair of light blue trousers instead of the long, flowing once-white robe he usually wore. He was bent over some kind of amazing contraption that Meena could not find a word for, it looked so complicated. And even as she looked, the object went click and whir-r and gr-r-r, and bulbs flashed all the colours she knew, and some she didn't, and something like a little toy windmill on the top spun rapidly, and a branch protruding out of the trunk went round and and round slowly, and a small light at the end of it blinked red, then green, then red again.

Meena was mesmerized. She stared at the machinery until the bending figure came upright and turned.

"Oh, I didn't see you come, Meena," Zeppi lied.

"Zeppi!" she exclaimed, "that is you? And what is all that — that, business?" She pointed a shaking hand.

"What business Meena?" He spoke mildly, and waved his hand and the machine stopped.

Meena took a tentative step forward.

"Stop!" Zeppi commanded. "Don't come one inch closer, else you would drop dead before you could say Jack Robinson!"

Meena stumbled back quickly. "What it is, Zeppi?"

"It's just a machine. Ain't you seen machines before? Ain't machine is the fashion in Tacarigua these days?"

"And what this one do?"

"Anything."

"It really look as if it could do anything!" She made a nervous sound like a laugh.

"For example, it say that Jaldo have to go hospital. That's what you come to find out, not so?"

"But how you know and only this morning I heard!"

"My machine. It could tell past, present, future, pluperfect and infinitive too."

"Don't send Jaldo hospital, Zeppi! Do something to stop it!"

"I can't do a thing, girl. All my powers gone inside the machine, and you can't change what it decide to do."

"I bring a fowl for you! I left it outside. And I will bring a dollar on payday."

"It don't matter if you bring all the money in the world."

Meena started to cry.

"That don't help either," he said.

"I got no future then!"

"Oh, Jaldo will come back better," Zeppi said, "and then the both of you will prosper, and have the biggest house in the village, and the overseer will turn Jaldo into foreman over all the others."

"That's for the future, but what going to happen now, how I will manage on my own?"

"The sugar estate will give you some money to help until Jaldo able to work. Zeppi turned his back on her and switched the machine on. He acted as if she were not there, fiddling with knobs and switches, and after a minute or so she backed out, as if she did not dare to turn away from the machine.

Before the day was out Meena had given Zeppi's machine all the free and sensational advertisement he expected. By the time she got to Lutchman's shop word had spread to every labourer or woman she met on their way to work in the canefields, and the account was exaggerated and expanded from lip to lip, and there were fierce arguments which was the truthful version.

Lutchman had his own problems when Meena came in bursting with the news. Some time in the night the shop had been broken into, and the drawer in which he kept his money robbed of twenty dollars. To Lutchman that was a lot of money. In the small village where they all knew each other, there was no need for police: once a month a constable rode a bicycle through the village and the children ran after him, it was such an unusual sight. On the rare occasion when the law was broken a detective or policeman had to be brought in, and no one could remember when that had last happened.

Lutchman was in a bad mood. Meena did not get a chance to talk until he had voiced his opinion about the unknown rogue and vagabond and vowed he would have justice if he had to call in the whole police force in Trinidad.

"I don't want to hear no stupidness about any machine," he grumbled, half-listening to Meena. "It's them machines I have here what must make some thief think I am a millionaire."

"But you don't see, Lutchman? Zeppi could help you catch the thief!"

"Zeppi losing his powers, Meena, everybody know that."

"It's this machine he got. It could do anything! You should see it Lutchman, you never see anything like it in your life!"

"I seen him come back from cityside the other day, toting a big load. Must of been that."

"If you ask me that thing come from over the seas, I don't think they could make machine like that in Trinidad. Anyway," Meena took up the pound of flour she had bought, "it could be somebody outside the village what rob the shop, you know. Zeppi machine would know. All them lights flashing all about, not even Carnival-time I ever seen anything like it." Her voice droned on as she left the shop.

Lutchman didn't have anything to lose by visiting the obeahman.

It would save a great deal of time and bother if the matter could be solved by Zeppi. And it was not extraordinary for him to shut the shop for a short while to attend to other things.

Lutchman was the last person Zeppi expected to see.

"Ah," he greeted the shopkeeper, "some trouble in the shop? All roads lead to Zeppi in the end."

"What trouble?" Lutchman was panting from the climb.

Zeppi waved vaguely. "You not just taking a stroll in the hot sun."

"Where this machine I hear about?" They were standing in the entrance and Zeppi was blocking his view.

"It taking a rest," Zeppi said solemnly.

"It could catch a thief?" Lutchman asked bluntly.

"It could catch a thief, catch cold, catch ball — anything."

Lutchman sorted. "All I interested in is who thief my twenty dollars from the shop last night."

"Easy as kissing hand."

"Go on, then. Show me."

"Hold your horses. That's a big job. How much you paying?"

"Let's see it work first."

"Five dollars down, Lutchman."

"Only if it work."

"You got to give me time to organize." Zeppi was thinking what a wonderful opportunity it was to display his machine. "Suppose I come to the shop tonight and pick out the thief from the crowd?"

"I don't care how you do it, as long as we get results." It was only when Lutchman had gone that Zeppi realised he had put himself in one hell of a position. Obsessed with reinstating his status, it did not occur to him that the identity of the thief was as much a mystery to him as Lutchman. This trial was going to make or break him, no bluff or mumbling of incantation or lighting a fire to poke in the smoke and ashes for an answer. Failure could have him packing and making races out of Tacarigua before the dawn of a new day, when he might be jeered at and stoned to accelerate his departure.

He was sitting on the step, in a shady spot from the westering sun, wondering if he could pretend at the last minute that some component in the machine was not functioning properly, when he saw Felix coming up the hill. Late gambling and drinking had him out of shape and he was exhausted when he arrived, sweeping his hand across his forehead and flicking the perspiration away.

Without waiting to catch his breath he panted: "Zeppi! I hear you catch the thief who rob Lutchman!"

"Yeah," Zeppi muttered.

"And you going to expose him in the shop tonight."

"Sure. I wish it was full moon, though." It wouldn't do any harm to set up little glimmers of doubt. "My new machine behaving cantankerous today, too. Altogether, when I say 'sure,' I don't mean sure-sure, you know what I mean?"

26

"Ah, you always trying to puzzle up a man!" Felix sat down next to the obeahman, a little nervously. "Listen Zeppi, I got something to tell you."

The shop was more crowded than on the day of the x-ray unit. Even the children were allowed out, and were playing whoop in the shadows of the shop. The machine was covered over with a piece of tarpaulin and Zeppi stood near to it, waiting patiently for Meena to finish recounting the story of her preview, as she was the only one who had seen it. Zeppi, if he felt any twinge of doubt how the proceedings would go, did not show it in his relaxed manner.

"Finish with that, Meena," Lutchman said, "you only holding up the works." He raised his voice. "All right, everybody, keep quiet, let Zeppi take the floor!"

Gradually the hubbub died down, and they formed a nervous semi-circle around the machine, but keeping a cautious distance away. Zeppi pushed his head under the tarpaulin and waited. Sure enough there was an impatient cry: "Come on, Zeppi, we waiting!" He threw the tarpaulin off, the machine already in operation.

They watched in awe as the colours flashed about and Zeppi touched a hundred switches and pulled levers and handles. A round ball with arms sticking out of it spun around and around, the machine hummed and whirred, and when Zeppi touched a certain button it made a sound like someone sawing wood. And to crown it all — something Meena had never mentioned — a hidden tape recorder played futuristic music.

"Jesus Christ," a woman cried, "it must be a monster from space!"

"What about the thief?" Lutchman demanded. "You got him inside the machine?"

Nobody laughed, because why not? Lutchman had a talking machine, so why couldn't the great Zeppi have the thief inside the contraption.

"Now Lutchman," Zeppi said, "the machine reading your mind, and it appear to more interested in getting your money back than catching the thief. True or not true?"

"True," Lutchman admitted.

"Watch." Zeppi flicked a switch. Out of the side of the machine a five-dollar bill appeared, then another, then two more. The first one pushed the other and they all fell on the floor.

"Oh jeez and ages!" Somebody cried, "Zeppi machine could make money too!"

There was a babble of exclamations and remarks as Lutchman scrambled up the money.

Zeppi switched off the machine and folded his arms. There was a loud chorus of protest.

"Come on Zeppi, put it back on!"

"Who is the thief?"

"Yes, that's what we want to know, who is the thief?"

Felix waved his arms wildly and shouted: "What's the matter with you-all? Lutchman select to get back his money, and he got it back, who care who's the thief?"

"We want to know the thief," Rosa cried. "That's what we all come for!"

Felix gave her an angry shove. "Shut your interfering mouth! You can't see Zeppi do what he say he was going to do?"

But the crowd was roused. There was no more awe and fear, only disappointment and anger. They began to make nasty remarks, and one man went so far as to put his hand on the machine, and nothing happened, no bolt of lightning struck him dead. Others came closer, hemming in the obeahman.

"All right!" Zeppi shouted. "Back off! I could make this machine blow up and kill everybody here tonight!"

"Do it, then," a voice called insolently, and there were cries of "Yes, blow it up let we see!"

"Jaldo want to know how long he got to stay in hospital," Felix said.

"I rather we catch the thief," Jaldo told Zeppi.

"Okay, okay." Zeppi raised his arms for order. "Lutchman, get some little pieces of paper and write down the name of everybody in the shop. Yours too, and mines. Also, leave one piece of paper blank, in case it's somebody outside the village."

As the crowd turned their attention to Lutchman, Felix grabbed Zeppi's shoulder and whispered harshly, "You and me make a bargain, Zeppi!"

"The bargain good, Felix. Leave it to me."

"I only hope you know what you doing," Felix growled.

Lutchman brought the tlips of paper and gave Zeppi. "I put down mines, and yours too, just as you say," he said.

Zeppi put the papers in the machine and set it going. Now the villagers were splitting up and moving apart, each suspicious of the other, as if the one caught standing next to the thief would be equally guilty.

A slip of paper came out and Zeppi stopped the machine and held it up for a moment for all to see, then peered at it. A look of consternation crossed his face.

"Read it Zeppi, who it say?" Lutchman asked.

"Nothing. The paper is blank. Is just as I thought, it's somebody from outside the village."

Before he could do anything Lutchman snatched it away, crying, "Let me see!" He glanced quickly at the slip. "It got a name on it, Zeppi, you lying!"

Felix made a grab for it but Rosa held on to his arm.

"Read it Lutchman!" She cried.

"It's Zeppi! It got Zeppi name on it!" Lutchman doubled up in laughter. Rosa took the slip from him and waved it about. "It's true! I see Zeppi name!"

"Must be a simple mistake," Zeppi shouted. "I think I press the wrong button!"

But the slip was passing from hand to hand and they were all holding their sides, tears streaming down their faces as they rolled and staggered about the shop.

"One thing Zeppi could do," Meena gasped, hanging on to Rosa for support. "If he can't work obeah, at least he could make we laugh. I going to dead with laughing tonight!"

Zeppi began to dismantle the machine quickly and examine the interior in a bid to save face. But it was a hopeless situation for him. His moment of glory was gone, there was nothing he could do or say. He would have to pack up and move South and set up business in a village near the oilfields, where the workers had more money. He would have to act quickly while they were helpless with laughing.

And after all, when he came to think of it, he was still master of the situation in a way, for they still didn't know who the thief was. He could even afford a chuckle himself as he realised his disappearance might lead them to believe that he was the culprit. He knew Felix would never breathe a word.

NEIL BISSOONDATH

INSECURITY

"We're very insecure in this place, you know." Alistair Ramgoolam crossed his fat legs and smiled beatifically, his plump cheeks, gouged by bad childhood acne, quivering at the effect his words had had. "You fly down here, you look around, you see a beautiful island, sun, coconut trees, beaches. But I live here and I see a different reality, I see the university students parading Marx and Castro on the Campus, I see more policemen with guns, I see people rioting downtown, I see my friends running away to Vancouver and Miami. So you can see, we are very insecure down here. That is why I want you to put the money your company owes me into my Toronto bank account. It is my own private insurance. The bank will notify me the money has been deposited and the government here won't notice a thing."

Their business concluded, the visitor pocketed Mr. Ramgoolam's account number and stood ready to leave. He asked to use the phone. "I'd like to call a taxi. My flight leaves early in the morning."

"No, no." Mr. Ramgoolan gestured impatiently with his plump arm. "Vijay will drive you into town. You're staying at the Hilton, not so?"

The visitor nodded.

"Vijay! Vijay!" Mr. Ramgoolam's silver hair — stirred, the visitor noticed, by the slightest movement — jumped as if alive.

Vijay's voice rattled like a falling can as it came in irritated response from the bowels of the house. "Coming, Pa, coming."

The tick-tock of Vijay's table tennis game continued and Mr. Ramgoolam, chest heaving, bellowed, "Vijay!"

Still smiling beatifically, Mr. Ramgoolam turned to his visitor and said, "So when you'll be coming back to the islands again?"

The visitor shrugged and smiled. "That depends on the company. Not for a long time probably."

"You like Yonge Street too much to leave it again soon, eh?" Mr. Ramgoolam chuckled. The visitor smiled politely.

Vijay, rake thin and wild-eyed, crawled into the living room.

Mr. Ramgoolam saw the visitor to Vijay's sports car, the latest model on the road. "You won't forget to get the letter to my son, eh? Remember, it's Markham Street, the house number and phone number on the envelope. You won't forget, eh?"

"I won't forget," the visitor said. They shook hands.

Mr. Ramgoolam was back in his house before the gravel spat up by the tires of the car had settled. He followed the tail-lights through a heavily burglar-proofed window — Vijay was speeding again, proba-

30

bly showing off; he'd need another talking to. Nodding ponderously, he muttered, "We're very insecure in this place, yes, very insecure."

Alistair Ramgoolam was a self-made man who thought back with pride to his poor childhood. He credited this poverty with preventing in him the aloofness he often detected in his friends: a detachment from the island, a sneering view of its history. He had, he felt, a fine grasp on the island, on its history and its politics, its people and its culture. He had developed a set of "views" and anecdotes which he used to liven up parties. It distressed him that his views and anecdotes rarely had the desired effect, arousing instead only a deadpan sarcasm. He had written them down and had them privately published in a thin volume. Except for those he'd given away as gifts, all five hundred copies were collecting dust in cardboard boxes under the table-tennis board.

Mr. Ramgoolam had seen the British when they were the colonial masters and he had attended the farewell ball for the last British governor. He had seen the Americans arrive with the Second World War, setting up their bases on large tracts of the best agricultural land; and he had seen the last of them leave, the Stars and Stripes tucked securely under the commander's arm, more than twenty years after the end of the war. He had seen the British, no longer masters and barely respected, leave the island in a state of independence. And he had seen that euphoric state quickly degenerate into a carnival of radicals and madmen.

His life at the fringe of events, he felt, had given him a certain authority over and comprehension of the past. But the present, with its confusion and corruption, eluded him. The sense of drift nurtured unease in Mr. Ramgoolam.

He would always remember one particular day in late August, 1969. He had popped out of his air-conditioned downtown office to visit the chief customs officer at the docks. As an importer of foreign goods and wines, Mr. Ramgoolam made it his business to keep the various officials who controlled the various entry stamps happy and content. On that day, he was walking hurriedly past the downtown square when a black youth, hair twisted into worm-like pigtails, thrust a pink leaflet into his unwilling hands. It was a socialist tract, full of new words and bombast. Mr. Ramgoolam had glanced irritatedly at it, noticed several spelling mistakes, crumpled it up, and threw it on the sidewalk. Then he remembered he was a member of the Chamber of Commerce Keep-Our-City-Clean committee and he picked it up. Later that evening he found it in his pants pocket. He smoothed it out, read it, and decided it was nothing less than subversion and treason. At the next party he attended, he expounded his views on socialism. He was told to stop boring everyone.

Not long after the party, riots and demonstrations — dubbed "Black Power" by the television and the newspaper — occurred in the streets. Mr. Ramgoolam's store lost a window pane and the walls were scribbled with "Socialism" and "Black Communism." The words bedevilled the last of Mr. Ramgoolam's black hairs into the mass of silver.

As he watched the last black stripe blend in, Mr. Ramgoolam realized that, with an ineffectual government and a growing military, one night could bring the country a change so cataclysmic that the only issue would be rapid flight. And failing that, poverty, at best.

He had no desire to return to the moneyless nobility of his childhood: pride was one thing, stupidity quite another, and Alistair Ramgoolam was acutely aware of the difference.

He began looking for ways of smuggling money out of the island to an illegal foreign bank account. A resourceful man, he soon found several undetectable methods: buying travellers' cheques and bank drafts off friends, having money owed him by foreign companies paid into the illegal account, buying foreign currency from travellers at generous rates of exchange. His eldest son was attending university in Toronto, so it was through him that Mr. Ramgoolam established his account.

The sum grew quickly. Mr. Ramgoolam became an exporter of island foods and crafts. deflating the prices he reported to the island's government and inflating those he charged the foreign companies. The difference was put into the Toronto account. Every cent not spent on his somewhat lavish lifestyle was poured into his purchases of bank drafts and travellers' cheques.

The official mail service, untrustworthy and growing more expensive by the day, was not entrusted with Mr. Ramgoolam's correspondence with his son. Visitors to or from Toronto, friend or stranger, were asked to perform favours.

Over the years, with a steadily developing business and ever-increasing foreign dealings, Mr. Ramgoolam's account grew larger and larger, to more than forty thousand dollars.

He contemplated his bankbooks with great satisfaction. Should flight be necessary — and the more time passed, the more Mr. Ramgoolam became convinced it would — there would be something to run to beyond bare refuge.

The more insecure he saw his island becoming, the more secure he himself felt. From this secure insecurity a new attitude, one of which he had never before been aware, arose in him. The island of his birth, on which he had grown up and where he had made his fortune, was transformed by a process of mind into a kind of temporary home. Its history ceased to be important, its present turned into a fluid holding pattern which would eventually give way. The confusion had been prepared for, and all that was left was the enjoyment that could be squeezed out of the island between now and then. He could hope for death here but his grandchildren, maybe even his children, would continue the emigration which his grandfather had started in India, and during which the island had proved, in the end, to be nothing more than a stopover.

When the Toronto account reached fifty thousand dollars, Mr. Ramgoolam received a letter from his eldest son. He reminded his father that Vijay would be coming to Toronto to study and that the fifty thousand dollars was lying fallow in the account, collecting interest, yes, but slowly. Wouldn't it be better to invest in a house? This would mean that Vijay — Mr. Ramgoolam noticed his eldest son had discreetly left himself out — would not have to pay rent and, with the rapidly escalating property prices in Toronto, a modest fifty-thousand-dollar house could be resold later at a great profit.

His first reading of the letter brought a chuckle to Mr. Ramgoolam's throat. His independent-minded son, it seemed, was looking for a way of not paying rent. But then he felt a ripple of quiet rage run through him: his son had always made an issue of being independent, of making it on his own. Paying for the privilege, Mr. Ramgoolam thought, was the first requisite of independence. He put the suggestion out of his mind.

Later that night, just before bed, he read the letter aloud to his wife. This had long been their custom. She complained continually of "weakness" in the eyes. As he lay in bed afterwards, the words "great profit" stayed with him.

His wife said, "You going to buy it?"

He said, "Is not such a bad idea. I have to think."

When he awoke at four the next morning for his usual Hindu devotions, Mr. Ramgoolam's mind was made up. He walked around the garden picking the dew-smothered flowers with which he would garland the deities in his private prayer room and, breathing in the cool, fresh air of the young dawn's semi-light, he became convinced that the decision was already blessed by the beauty of the morning.

After a cold shower, Mr. Ramgoolam draped his fine cotton dhoti around his waist and prayed before his gods, calling their blessings onto himself, his wife, his sons, and the new house soon to be bought, cash, in Toronto. It was his contention that blessed business dealings were safer than unblessed ones.

He spent the rest of the morning writing a letter to his son, giving instructions that before any deals were made he was to be consulted. He didn't want any crooked real estate agent fooling his son, Toronto sophisticate or not. He also warned that the place should be close enough to Vijay's school that he wouldn't have to travel too far: a short ride on public transportation was acceptable but his son should always remember that it was below the station of a Ramgoolam to depend on buses and trains.

That was an important point, Mr. Ramgoolam thought. It might force his independent son to raise his sights a little. He probably used public transportation quite regularly in Toronto, whereas here on the island he would not have heard of sitting in a bus next to some sweaty farmer. The letter, Mr. Ramgoolam hoped, would remind his eldest son of the standards expected of a member of his family.

The letter was dispatched that evening with the friend of a friend of a friend who just happened to be leaving for Toronto.

A week passed and Mr. Ramgoolam heard nothing from his son. He began to worry: if *he* were buying a house, you could be sure *he'd* have found a place and signed the deal by now. That son of his just had no business sense: didn't he know that time was money? A week could mean the difference of a thousand dollars! Mr. Ramgoolam said to his wife, "I just wish he'd learn to be independent on somebody else's money."

He was walking in the garden worrying about his money and kicking at the grass when Vijay shouted from the house, "Pa, Pa! Toronto calling."

Mr. Ramgoolam hurried in, his cheeks jiggling. "Hello." It was the real estate agent calling.

The operator said, "Will you accept the charges?"

Accept the charges? Mr. Ramgoolam was momentarily unsettled. "No." He slammed the phone down. He glared at Vijay sitting at the dining table. "What kind of businessman he is anyway? Calling collect. He's getting my money and he expects me to pay for his business call? He crazy or what, eh?" Incensed, he ran out into the garden. Every few minutes, Vijay could hear him muttering about "cheapness."

The telephone rang again half an hour later.

This call was from his son and, luckily, not collect. The first thing Mr. Ramgoolam said was, "Get rid of that cheap agent. I don't trust him. Get someone else."

The son agreed. Then he asked his whether his father would be willing to go above fifty thousand, to, say, sixty or sixty-five. Only such a sum would assure a good house in a proper location. Less would mean a good house, yes, but along way on public transportation for Vijay.

Mr. Ramgoolam pictured Vijay riding on some rickety bus with a smelly fish vendor for company. He broke out in a cold sweat. "Now wait a minute . . . awright, awright, sixty or sixty-five. But not a cent more. And close the deal quickly. Time is money, you know."

Time dragged by. Nothing was heard from Toronto for a week. Mr. Ramgoolam began to worry. What was that no-good son of his up to now? Wasting time as usual, probably running off somewhere being independent.

Another week went by and Mr. Ramgoolam began brooding over the house in Toronto. He couldn't get his mind off it. He stopped going to the office. Not even prayer seemed to ease his growing doubts. Wasn't it better to have the cash safely in the bank, slowly but surely collecting its interest? And what about Vijay? The money for his schooling was to have come from that account: now he'd have to take money with him, and Mr. Ramgoolam hadn't counted on that. Above all, the house was going to cost ten to fifteen thousand more than the Toronto account contained; that was a lot of money to smuggle out. Would it mean a mortgage? He hated mortgages and credit. He hated owing. Buy only when you could pay: it was another of his convictions.

After three more days and a sleepless night, Mr. Ramgoolam eased himself out of bed at 3:30 a.m. He might as well pray. It always helped, eased the mind however little.

There was very little light that morning and the flowers he collected were wilted and soggy. He stubbed his toe on a stone and cursed, softly, in Hindi. The cold shower felt not so much refreshing as merely cold.

He prayed, his dhoti falling in careless folds, his gods sad with their colourless flowers.

When he finished he wrote a quick letter to his son, ordering him to leave all the money in the bank and to forget about buying a house. He couldn't afford it at the present time, he said.

He signed it and sealed it. He wondered briefly whether he should telephone or telegram but decided they were both too expensive. The next problem was to find someone who was going to Toronto. That was easy: the representative of his biggest Toronto client, the one staying at the Hilton, would be coming to his house this evening to finalize a deal and to get the Toronto account number. He could take the letter.

Five days passed and Mr. Ramgoolam heard nothing from his eldest son. Once more he began to worry. Couldn't the fool call to say he'd got the letter and the money was safe? He spent the morning in bed nursing his burning ulcer.

On the morning of the sixth day the call came.

"Hell, Pa?" His son's voice was sharp and clear, as if he were calling from across the street. "You're now the proud owner of a house in Toronto. The deal went through yesterday. It's all finalized."

Mr. Ramgoolam's jaw fell open. His cheeks quivered. "What? You didn't get my letter?"

"You mean the one the company rep brought up? Not yet. He just called me last night. I'm going to collect the letter this evening, before the ballet."

"Be-be-be-fore the ballet?" Mr. Ramgoolam ran his pudgy fingers down the length of his perspiring face. He could feel his heart thumping heavily against the fat in his chest.

"Yes, I'm going to the ballet tonight. Good news about the house, eh? I did exactly as you told me, Pa. I did it as quickly as possible. Time is money, as you always say."

"Yes-yes," said Mr. Ramgoolam. "Time is money, son, time is money. We're very insecure in this place, you know."

His son said, "What?"

"Nothing." Mr. Ramgoolam ran his hand, trembling through his hair. "Goodbye." He replaced the receiver. The wooden floor seemed to dance beneath him and, for a moment, he had a sense of slippage, of life turning to running liquid. He saw his son sitting in the living room of the Toronto house — sitting, smiling, in a room Mr. Ramgoolam knew to be there, but the hardened outlines of which he could not distinguish — and he suddenly understood how far his son had gone. Just as his father had grown distant from India; just as he himself had grown even further from the life that, in memory, his father had represented and then, later in life, from that which he himself had known on the island, so too had his eldest son gone beyond. Mr. Ramgoolam had been able to picture the money sitting in the bank, piles of bills; but this house, and his son sitting there with ballet tickets in his hand: this was something softer, hazier, less graspable. He now saw himself as being left behind, caught between the shades of his father and, unexpectedly, of his son. And he knew that his insecurity, until then always in the land a round him, in the details of life daily lived, was now within him. It was as if his legs had suddenly gone hollow, two shells of utter fragility.

There was only one thing left, one thing to hold on to. He hurried to his room and, brushing his wife aside, dressed quickly. Then he swallowed two hefty gulps of his stomach medicine and called out to Vijay to drive him to the office.

AUSTIN CLARKE

GIVE IT A SHOT

When he left home at seven in the morning for work in the Department of Transportation, the Drivers' Examination Section, his wife was still in bed. He was glad she didn't have to lift overweight patients and empty bedpans and watch people die today. Yesterday on her shift she watched three old women die, she told him. But today she was at home. And it pleased him. She was a wife, a housewife; and he felt like a man. He felt she was right to make him work harder and get the promotion which harder work would bring. She was right to urge him to get the part-time job at night and help them get out of the apartment in the Ontario housing project where they'd lived for ten years. She told him almost every morning when he left, and every evening when he got home tired from the Department of Transportation, that she wanted to live far from the welfare families and the growing number of West Indian immigrants who were moving into the project. Their cooking bothered her, she told him. She wanted to *live*. And live in a house.

Every evening she bugged him about her girl friends who had moved away already. "And some of them are even Jamaicans," she said, "so why we can't get ahead like them?"

He felt good leaving her in bed on this blood-freezing morning. Things were tough. He needed time to think. Time to think of getting her into a better residential district. Perhaps a house in the East End, in the Beaches area where the successful people were moving. But this morning, at least, she was a wife *and* a housewife; and for the moment he was the breadwinner. He always wanted to be the breadwinner. But his job showed no prospects to finance that chauvinism. This evening when he got home he would lay his cards on the table.

He settled himself comfortably at his desk. A member of his section was home sick, so he was in charge today. He had power. He was the supervisor. Even though it was for one day, he alone would decide the fate of the applicants. He could fail them or pass them.

Before lunch he had passed five persons. One or two he could have flunked. But his wife was at home. A housewife; and he liked that. If even for one day. Yesterday he had failed ten persons. Eight of them were West Indians. His wife went to work yesterday. He had dropped her off in front of the hospital emergency entrance. And that evening she announced she had to visit her Jamaican friend, May. "She's showing me her house tonight." He had grunted. "She doesn't even have a man." That was all she said, and then she left.

A young Jamaican sits before him now. The Jamaican's head is covered by a black, red and green woollen tam-o'-shanter. He wonders if he's Jewish. And to himself he swears: I won't be letting you loose on the decent people of this city, not today, boy! His wife had slammed the apartment door, and off she went to visit May. He heard her high heels clumping down the metal stairs. And from six floors above, he heard her slam the car door. When she drove off, he thought of the repair bill. The car was old. She wanted a house: he wanted a new car. He saw the gravel skidding behind her in the parking lot, and he thought of all the greasy-haired kids he had kept off the road. He had failed them by just looking at their long hair. Thank God I had the foresight to spot them early . . .

The Jamaican sits silent and threatening in front of him. The red, black and green of his woollen cap bothers him. I'm gonna keep you waiting, buster. You people got no patience or no manners, or respect for anybody. I can't understand why you people're in so much hurry...

He himself was a patient man. And all his life he had respected his superiors. He was even satisfied to remain a private in the Royal Canadian Scots Reserve Guards. It took him three years to be promoted. And it would take time to save and buy a house. It had taken him so many Thursday evenings to learn the new drills and the new weapons, and he was a man who had served overseas in the last war. It was as if he was learning all over again how to master the Royal-Sal-ute-Pre-sent-Arrrms! But by God, he got it! And he had been a proud private.

Why can't this bastard have patience? And why didn't May wait a little longer to buy her house, and now have my wife wife bitching and bitching? He was a patient man. Last year they made him corporal. In parades, with spit and polish, even if the rain came down and made plastic of his stiff khaki uniform, he knew the virtue of patience; and respect demanded that he remain standing at attention, with only the starch of his loyalty in his stance. The Queen was visiting Toronto at the time.

He was Scottish by descent. He felt he was more loyal than the burly West Indian sergeant at the top of the line. Somewhere in a book he had seen an inscription, *James, King of England and of Scotland*. It didn't say one damn thing about King of the West Indies.

The Jamaican begins to whistle a tune. With his car key or some other key, he cleans dirt from his thumbnails. These goddamn people! You can wait till I call my wife . . .

The telephone was ringing a long time and he imagined her slipping out of bed in the long, long nightgown that made her look like a wet zebra. I never liked it, its pattern or its sleek silkiness; and now she'd be putting on her slippers and cursing him because he couldn't afford broadloom for the cold floor.

But I'm doing my best. The whole country's in a mess, and I don't have no power to change that. All these goddamn strikes, and all these immigrants writing letters to the papers complaining, and living next door. . . Doesn't she hear the goddamn phone ringing? . . . Her entire salary went to buy Canada Savings Bonds and clothes . . . She would be in the kitchen by now, standing beside the fridge with her left hand holding the red wall phone which she herself chose; and by now she's wiping the sleep out of her eyes with her right hand and trying not to smear her mascara which she sleeps with . . . What a kid! I know that kid like the back of my hand! Love her too . . .

He became lost in his thoughts, in his life, in his world, in the seductive ringing of the telephone; and the monotony of the ringing made him forget the Jamaican.

He looked up at the Jamaican and told him, "You're okay." His wife had not answered. The Jamaican sat upright, as if the two words were jabs to his stomach. "This driving permit you're getting is a great privilege. *Not* a right. This country gives you this privilege to drive. So remember that." The Jamaican smiled and said, "Right on!" He held one hand up, and in a flash the hand became a fist. "Right on!" A smile changed his face and the whitest teeth he ever saw were grinning at him; and the Jamaican walked out of the office as if he was doing the boogaloo. He liked the Jamaican, but he refused to allow himself to feel soft towards him.

All of a sudden his mind went back to the telephone call to his wife. He was sad and alone and unsure of himself. And his insecurity made him sullen and malevolent. Another murderer, another maniac I've just let loose on society. He had given him a chance. It's a long shot, but what the hell!

The morning moved fast. He thought of a beer and a hamburger for lunch. He was obsessed by his work and by the feeling of responsibility it gave him. He wanted to surprise her by asking her to lunch, to that place she liked so much, that place that cooked that soul-food thing. That was another thing she was getting into recently. She and those goddamn exotic foods and exotic people! Wonder if she changed her mind and went to work, after all?

He made up his mind to serious consider the part-time job at night. Christ, I'm still better off than Bob, poor bastard.

Almost every Monday evening religiously, Bob, a neighbour on the fifth floor in his apartment building, would be sitting in his kitchen talking about the woman he married. "That bitch," Bob called her. He took refuge at the racetrack. The weekends and his wife took such a toll on Bob's face, and on his performance at work, that it reflected in his luck at the track. And his losses were heaviest on the weekends. Bob used to work with him in the Department of Transportation, but when the economy took a nose dive and promotion was not forthcoming, he left this civil service job and announced he was going to make a living off the track.

No, he had nothing to complain about. The kid's okay. And that trip to the West Indies she's always bugging me about, well, if . . . "My girl friend May bought her ticket last week . . ." Well, tonight he would give her the goddamn money for the trip to Jamaica. "To the Barbados, Grenada, Antigua, South America, Cuba, any goddamn place, kid!" He could hardly wait to get home and make it up with her, doing all the things he had promised. He felt a strong spasm of love. She was his kid. His queen.

And when he left work, custom guided his car to a stop beside the fire hydrant in front of the main entrance of the hospital. Every day after work he would sit in this place to wait for her, and listen to the report of traffic rushing and bounding on the Don Valley Parkway, exactly where he had to travel to get home; and he would curse the city politicians and the town planners who did not give a damn about him. And here he was, protecting the city from the greasy-haired kids and immigrants who drove like maniacs on the same Don Valley.

This afternoon he remained parked illegally by the fire hydrant for a long time, thinking about the part-time job. His attention was taken up by news of accidents and traffic jams. And he would have sat longer if May hadn't come out and noticed him. "What the hell you doing here, man?" She held her bust through the window while he looked at the lace of her brassiere and smelled the enticing perfume and saw the rusty safety pin beside the flowers embroidered on her bra. "Pat, your wife not working today, man. She call in sick. She take off three days. Pat, you ain't know?" And she laughed the loud, happy laugh he had heard so often on the telephone. "So, when you coming to see my new place, eh?"

All of a sudden he couldn't smell her perfume. And he lost sight of the safety pin and the caution on the radio news about heavy traffic on the Don Valley Parkway. He wished he could catch up with that Jamaican whom her had passed. Anywhere, anyplace, anytime, I see that bastard, I'm gonna take that permit outa his goddamn hands!

The Don Valley was not crowded. He didn't know what that bastard on the radio was talking about. You can't trust any goddamn person these days! So he pressed his foot flat on the gas pedal, swung from the slow lane into the middle and straight across into the fast lane without using his indicator. A car he had just missed blew its horn. *Ma*niacs! Through his rear-view mirror he saw them. He decided they were West Indians. *Goddamn maniacs! Bastards! Illegal immigrants! Fuck off!* He punched his fist on his car horn, and the frightened driver and his two passengers were left in a cloud of smoke and vapour.

When he reached home, he slammed on the brakes and turned off the ignition at the same time. The old car shot forward, and then died. He turned off the lights and sat for a while. He got out and looked up, trying to identify his apartment, searching among dozens for the light in his windows. His wife had placed a stubby plant on the windowsill. He hated that stubby plant. One of her nurse friends had given it to her. Those stupid bastards who're foolish enough to marry her girl friends! They need a tough bugger like me to control them . . . He did not see the plant; and he could not tell which lights were in in his apartment.

Bob was in the elevator. "Months now I been telling you to give up your job and come to the races. The biggest goddamn 100 per cent guaranteed investment in the world!" Two old ladies got into the elevator just before the doors closed. Bob modified his speech. "Made me a bundle today," he whispered. "Caught the Double too. Paid three bills." One old lady got out. "You're wasting time being a civil servant, Pat," he said in a louder voice. The old lady who remained was a Jamaican whom he had once seen at the track. "All these years he's working for the goddamn government. And for what?" The lady just smiled. "Me and him," he said, looking at Pat and then at the lady, "the two of us was in the war." She got off. "We fought in the goddamn war together. Where was any goddamn government? That goddamn . . ." He reached the fifth floor where he got off.

Pat remained in the humming elevator, with thoughts of the races and winning and making a down payment on a house from those winnings. Perhaps. Perhaps he should give it a shot one of these weekends.

The carpet on which he was walking was worn bare by the treading of many feet. That's another thing wrong with this building. Too many goddamn immigrants and children. The elevator had graffiti in it. The tiles in the lobby were broken. And more than once he thought he smelled urine in the elevator.

Did I turn off my car lights? I have so many goddamn things on my mind.

A couple of times last summer he had gone to the track with Bob and made a few bucks . . . But to make a living as a racetrack tout? No, I could never do that. I'm a veteran and a public servant.

The decisions he made to withhold driving permits from West Indians and the greasy-haired kids went without publicity. Not even his supervisor raised a finger. And nobody ever took a photograph or wrote a feature story on his public spiritedness. From his training in the war and, more recently, the weekly parades at the fort down Jarvis Street, he was fashioned into a stern man. A man of discipline. I know where every penny of my paycheque goes. I can trace every goddamn penny, and if I had more, I could trace them too . . .

His key was giving him trouble. There was no light coming from under his door. Was I right about that Jamaican fellow? The door swung open and he stood facing a black apartment. He closed the door and went back into the corridor. He could smell curry. He was sure he could smell urine too. He checked the number on the door. It was his apartment. So he opened it a second time, switched on the light and stood just inside the threshhold, a bit timidly, and stared at the rectangle of clean white paint where the red phone had been unscrewed, and at other squares and rectangles of dust and hair where furniture had once stood. And in each of these dimensions were four little dents in the softwood floor where chairs and tables, the stereo and the colour television had stood.

He's in the bathroom now. He sees the same dust and the same four sets of dents, heavier in one place and deeper because this spot represented the weight of their two bodies, tired after work, for six equally tired years, as she once told him.

The four rooms are stripped bare. But she's left the stubby plant on the windowsill in the kitchen.

The place is cold. There's one chair he finds in the kitchen. She probably remembered how tired I am at night. I need a drink . . . He opens the cupboard above the sink where he keeps his whisky. Dust and grains of sugar and flour and rice. And some black dots. The building was infested with mice and cockroaches. The kid bugged me all last week to get the super to spray this place . . . In the refrigerator, on the second shelf, is one beer and a parcel wrapped in tinfoil.

He searched for the bottle of whisky and couldn't find it. He became angry now to think that she had left a beer and had taken the bottle opener. All the cutlery was gone too. And the emptiness of the place made him hungrier than he was angry. He opened the bottle with his teeth. He sipped the beer. Something crossed his mind and he jerked his head and stood up, his thoughts racing like his old car. He rushed into the bathroom. He pushed his hand under the water tank of the toilet. When his hand touched the bundle there, he smiled and felt warmer. She had missed that. He unwrapped the Canadian flag and from amongst its folds a gun was revealed.

Every Sunday he cleaned the gun in his parked car in the nearby park. It was a souvenir from the war. After the building became integrated, he kept it loaded. Now he dropped the Canadian flag on the hard floor and stepped over it, holding the gun in his hand like a man who is prepared for an intruder.

He's in the kitchen again. Sitting on the upright wooden chair. In one hand is the gun. In the other is the chicken leg which was in the tinfoil. He takes a large bite out of the chicken, but he could be biting her or destroying her, so ferocious is the bite. He sits facing the stubby plant.

I was a damn fool to take that chance on that goddamn Jamaican. I was a damn fool to listen to this broad. I should have put my foot down, even in her ass, and told her where to get off. I shoulda been like the other men and stuffed that dead-end civil service job long time ago . . .

He got up. He watered the stubby plant with some of his beer. What am I beefing about? I've seen harder times. I was in the war. And I'm a loyal subject. I got a right to live off this goddamn country. I'm no fucking immigrant! This country owes me a goddamn living . . .

Never before had he seen so many people not at work in the middle of the day. He was at the track. No wonder there's so much unemploy-

42

ment! And so many West Indian immigrants. He would never have guessed from sitting at his desk in the Department of Transportation that the government had let in so many black people as immigrants. Christ, they're all here at the races.

Bob had succeeded in getting him to go to the track. Bob was a friend. He was very decent to him the night his wife left. He was surprised by his sympathy. Bob had sat with him all through that first night, looking at the stubby plant, commenting on its ugliness, and drinking the case of beer he had brought with him.

Bob turned to him now and said, "Look at these unemployed bastards, would ya?" The horses were coming through the tunnel. Bob looked over each one and made a stroke in his program. "See that one with the coloured groom? Put your money on him."

"On the groom?" He was enjoying himself.

"The horse, you bugger!"

Pat looked at the horse and then at the groom, and was sure he recognized the groom. "I had no idea there was so many goddamn Jamaicans in this racket!"

"Best goddamn grooms in the racket," Bob said, "those coloured boys are! You don't know this since you don't know horse racing, but the history of the great Kentucky Derby is the history of coloured jockeys. Now they've come from jockeys to being grooms. Let's give the 10-horse a shot."

Travelling in Bob's car on the way home that afternoon, Bob told him, "Tell ya what . . ." He was recapturing the excitement and victories he had had at the track. They were jammed in creeping traffic on the Don Valley. But he didn't care. Bob had given him three good tips, and he had won two hundred dollars, tax-free, as Bob liked to say. He had it in his pocket. Today was the third straight day he had taken off from work. Sick leave. He didn't give a damn. He would take another three days off. He didn't miss his wife.

"Tell ya what," Bob said again. "The super in our building's leaving. To go out west. They'll be looking for a super and I thought . . . So why don't you give it a shot?" Pat was finding the speeding cars fascinating. "Beats beating your brains out down at Transport," Bob told him. "Incidentally, I'm bringing a Jamaican buddy of mine to the poker game Saturday."

Next day on the way to the Woodbine racetrack, Bob told him, "Ya got it! I talked to the super, the super talked to the agent, and ya got it! Your war service came in handy. Goddamn, you're a free man now!"

They were driving in heavy holiday traffic and he was thinking of his luck and hardly said a word. He had never had so much money before. Cash in his pockets. He didn't have to face those greasy-haired kids . . .

"Sure thing!" he said.

Bob was startled. "You all right, Pat?"

"Sure thing! The Jamaican fellow and the poker game!"

"Ya got it!" Bob said.

Why didn't I throw that broad out on her ass years ago? A new life opened its pages to him in the excitement of the *Racing Form*. He and Bob stopped taking the common entrance. Valet parking and the clubhouse became commonplace now. They stopped drinking beer and sipped scotch instead. They quickly learned the sophistication of the clubhouse. And they grinned when they won, and gritted their teeth and tried to smile when they lost, and said, "We had to give it a shot!"

One day Pat found himself standing behind a well-dressed Jamaican at the betting wicket. He had heard the man talk. And when the man moved away, the computer print-out which was still on the machine said *$900.00* in red. He told the ticket seller, "Fifty dollars to win . . . on the same horse."

"You mean the 1-horse?"

Bob had given him the 5-horse. He took the ticket. His hand was shaking. He had to give it a shot. Nervously he headed back to Bob, sitting with two scotches.

"Did ya go with me on the 5-horse?"

The same well-dressed Jamaican approached their table. He slapped Bob on the back. "That 1-horse. Look at the form in the *Form* that that 1-horse got, mastah. *Cahn't* lose!" Pat felt stronger now. "I backed it to show. Nine hundred on the motherfucker." And he left just as abruptly, to see the race.

Bob underlined in red ballpoint the 5-horse's previous performances. He showed it to Pat, who wasn't attending. Bob then kissed his ticket. "If this 5-horse comes in at 13-to-one . . . Oh, he's the fellow, the poker fellow! . . . My trip to the Bahamas paid for. Christ, I'm gonna have me some broads in the sun!"

But Pat was committed elsewhere: that Thunderbird I put a hundred dollars on. I need only five hundred more by the weekend. Plus the rent money I borrowed which I have to put back this weekend too...

The first time, for almost a month, it had been real easy. But it was becoming more difficult. He had to make five hundred on this horse to repay two weeks' rent he had borrowed from the safe. When he got the job, the agent lectured him about keeping the accounts of the apartment building up-to-date and told him twice, "Keep the rent money safe in the office safe!" He had lost at the track and at the poker table all last week. And the Thunderbird . . . The 1-horse was the longest shot. If it came in, he would turn his fifty into five hundred, or five thousand . . . or five million, tax-free, as Bob liked to say. He felt safer betting with the Jamaican than with Bob. And he's a poker player too! Between this race and the poker game . . . lemme see, I should get back an even . . .

Bob was talking to him. "Let's watch this race and get some thrills for our money."

44

They went into the stands outside but every seat was taken. The space on the lawn in front of the stands was packed. "You were great last Sattadee night at the game. Shit, you hid that Ace in the hole and had everybody thinking you had only Ace-high . . . You musta pulled in four, five hundred bucks in that one pot . . ."

The horses were emerging from the tunnel. He looked at the 1-horse. A black groom was leading it. The groom looked into the stand in Pat's direction, recognized someone, and Pat saw him wink and heard him say, "*Cahn'* lose!" And Pat began to replace all the rent money he had borrowed. He stopped watching the horses. He looked at the people, and he loved the world. In his mind he did all the chores: cleaned the driveway, repaired an old lady's stove, fixed a young couple's fuse box and washed the elevators . . .

Those goddamn immigrants always pissing in the elevators! When he was a tenant he could look at all this filth and look away, even though he always grumbled about it. But now that he was the super, each speck of filth meant hours of hard work. If I was still with Transportation, I would flunk every one of them.

His eyes passed like a camera panning over the vast crowd murmuring with excitement before the race. His eyes rested on a woman. She was beautiful in a sensual way. Her hair was dyed blonde. Even from the back she looked sexy. She was well-dressed. The crowd was hushed. He looked at the starting gate and saw his horse. It had danced before him as it paraded in front of the people. Something wrenched his eyes from the horse back over the multitude of people to the woman. His heart stopped beating. He recognized her. "Look at that bitch!" It was his wife. Beside her was the well-dressed Jamaican who, like him, had backed the same horse. In all the years I knew that broad, she never even read the goddamn sports pages! And look at that bitch now! If I was still with Transportation, I would flunk every goddamn . . .

Minutes later, after the 1-horse had come in third and Bob was laughing and dancing and talking about screwing Bahamian women, Pat was trying to roll his ticket into a small ball and fire it and shoot his wife, the bitch! The first time he had seen her at the track, and he had lost! Now he saw her leap into the air when the tote board gave the results. The Jamaican was smiling. He saw him hand her the ticket, and she climbed the steps to the cashiers' wickets. He pushed through the crowd to cut her off. "Get outa my goddamn way, nigger!"

A black man was moving too slowly for him.

"Hey!" someone yelled. But he was losing patience. "Watch it, buster!" he told the man.

"No, you watch it, fellow!" The voice that spoke was a Scottish brogue, a rich brogue of rebuke. "I say!" But he was losing his wife in the crowd to a Jamaican, and he didn't give a damn about Scottish ancestry now. He was losing his temper too.

"Rass, man! To-rass!"

He lost his temper. She stopped. He turned around. In front of him was a man much like the Jamaican with the red, black and green woollen cap. Men like you didn't talk back to me when I was with Transportation. I had men like you in my hand, in my power . . . He thought of his wife in bed with the Jamaican.

"You sonofa*bitch*!"

"Rass, mahn! What you call I?"

"You heard me!"

The Jamaican rushed at him. A crowd gathered. Bob saw him and pulled him from the Jamaican. Silently the crowd witnessed their exchange of violence with words. And when it was finished, when the words stopped and left only the bad smell of feeling, the crowd surged to the large glass wall to see the horses entered in the next race.

Bob patted him on his shoulder to quell the spirit in him. Then he started to check his winnings, holding the twenty-dollar bills spread like a fan, like playing cards. "That poker game *tonight*! The Jamaican fellow's coming. I know he walks with more money than a bank." Bob pushed his money into his pocket. "What did I tell ya? Didn't I give ya the 5-horse? Didn't I give ya a big winner? Didn't I pick 'em for ya?"

Tenants came and dropped their rent cheques through the slot in the door. The office was closed. He watched them fall. He was cleaning his own apartment for the poker game, so he ignored them, just as he had earlier ignored the leaves he walked over up at Woodbine, leaves like the tickets of wrong bets discarded on the vast cement floor of the clubhouse. The trees at Woodbine were like gold at this time of year. He liked to drag his feet through their fallen colours of gold and russet. Someone was pressing his buzzer.

These goddamn tenants! Don't they think I have a life of my own? I'm tired cleaning up after them . . . A fat black woman past middle age stood facing him. He tried to imagine what she looked like naked. She was smiling. He became sorry for his thoughts.

"Mr. Pat, boy, I bring your rent since the office is closed." She came inside and sat down. "Lemme rest this weary body, boy. Work killing me. I don't know what keeping me in this cold place. Jamaica more better." She threw a cough drop into her mouth. "How you making out at the track? I hear you goes there every day."

"Canada's better than many places I know," he said. "Take the States, for instance . . ."

"Me, child? There? . . . I paying you one month in advance. Count it. Five hundred, eh?" He had ignored her comment about the races. Now he watched her as a smile came over her face. He thought he saw a sparkle in her eyes. "In all the time I living here, you's the most decent super ever put in charge o' this building. I would hate to see you leave." What was she telling him? "The place looking the most decentest it ever look!"

46

He smiled and shook her hand after giving her the receipt. Absent-mindedly he put the five hundred dollars in his pocket. He watched her walk slowly along the shining corridor, and then she started sneezing and had to hold onto the wall for support. He had just sprayed the corridor with Lysol. She looked back and waved at him. "Have a good night . . ." And he stood at the door and watched her slowly become smaller.

He was happy and warm and fresh and clean. The shower did him good. His mind was clear and deadly. They had been playing poker for many hours now, and he was still concentrating. The six of them, including the well-dressed Jamaican, were still around the aluminum table on which he had spread a white bed sheet. He looked at the clock beneath his Canadian flag, and the hands showed him it was long after midnight. "Let's send out for some Kentucky fried," he said.

"I could eat a horse, to-rass!" the Jamaican said. "And Bob here could buy chicken for the whole building, the way he been kicking ass tonight."

"Chicken? Shit! First thing tomorrow, Sattadee, I purchasing my ticket to the Bahamas. I'm through with you bastards."

"That 5-horse ran like a motherfucker, eh, Bob?"

"They should shoot that 1-horse," Pat said. They all laughed. "Well, I'll call for the Kentucky fried."

And he went into his bedroom where the phone was. He was happy. He poured a little of his scotch on the ugly stubby plant. He may even pay for the whole order. He sat on a pillow. He eased the pillow from under him the moment he sat down, and when he moved it aside he realized her had placed his gun there. He gave the order and the address. He got up and left the gun exposed on the bed. He poured some more scotch on the stubby plant, and as he did he cursed his wife; and he watered the stubby plant each time he thought of her. The plant was sturdier than he had thought. "In twenty minutes, gang," he announced when he rejoined them.

"Well, let's *deal*," the Jamaican said.

Bob started to sing "Brown Skin Gal." The Jamaican joined him. Bob changed to "Rum and Coca Cola."

"Let's make this the last game," he said.

"Let's make it a big one!" the Jamaican said. "To-rass. It's only bread."

Pat won the next three games. He was now completely out of debt. He could replace every outstanding rent payment he had borrowed. All of a sudden the Jamaican and he were the only two players left. The game was five card stud. The second cards were dealt. He had a King in the hole, and an Ace showing. Another King dropped in front of him. A four to the Jamaican. He could hear the others breathing hard. He bet twenty dollars as bluff. The Jamaican looked at a pair of fours that had just dropped in front of him, peeped at his hole card and said, "Let's have some fun. 'Ere tonight, gone to-rass tomorrow, bredder!" He stared at Pat. "See your twenty and raise you *one hundred* and twenty, bredder!" The breathing stopped.

"Good night, Irene," he began to whistle through his teeth. It was a rasping, annoying sound. "Shit, I took a shot."

The next card Pat got was a four. This bastard's four! He was silently ecstatic. It's the last game anyhow.

The Jamaican started to count out two thousand dollars. He dropped the pile on the table. Pat felt that if he could win this pot, he would not only replace all the rent money but would also buy the Thunderbird.

"How much bread you have in this place, bredder?"

Pat looked at the clock. He looked at the Canadian flag, focusing on the large Maple Leaf, red and sturdy like his Scottish ancestry. He refused to answer the Jamaican. The Jamaican repeated the question, this time with some venom in his voice. I'm not your goddamn brother.

"Fifty," the Jamaican called, dragging out his bet as he looked Pat full in the eyes, "and five hundred . . . Five hundred and fifty, bredder."

Pat had three hundred dollars in front of him. But he remembered the five hundred in his pocket from the kind black lady. He had another thirteen hundred inside, in a drawer where he kept the cash from the rent money when the office was closed. He kept it there near his gun until the agent came to collect it.

"Are you calling, bredder?"

All Pat could hear was the hoarseness in the man's voice. He felt a tug at his guts. The others started to breathe again, harder. And they were standing up. Then it became very quiet. Pat could hear the clock ticking. "I have *nine* hundred and fifty," he said. "I raise!" His voice dropped a decibel.

The Jamaican jumped up. His eyes were red. He stared at his cards. He stared at Pat's cards. He seemed to be looking right through the cards to their turned down faces. He was trying to remember something. He became tense. But there was anger in him too. He was concentrating on two cards which Pat had been dealt, trying to remember how he had bet when he got those cards. All of a sudden he broke wind. It was a loud, sharp, short blast.

"'Scuse me, bredder."

"You pass, or you fold, sonofa*bitch*?"

"Hell, no! I raise, man."

Pat could feel his feet dragging in leaves, and he could feel his guts in knots, and the fatigue of the long night brought a film to his eyes. He became cold. He got up and went into the bedroom. They heard a tap running. He came back, and without a word he counted two thousand dollars. He threw the bills on the table. They were like leaves. He imagined his fingers walking through them, gathering them all in.

48

I'm gonna take a trip myself . . . better still, put a down payment on a goddamn house, if that's what she still wants . . . He could see her in the long sleek silk zebra nightgown. He saw the Jamaican touching her and the zebra cloth. *But she's mine, sonofabitch!* His hands began to shake. He put them on his thighs under the table, while Bob checked the pot to see if it was correct. Bob was smiling. The Jamaican was smiling. Pat's hands were moving up and down his thighs. His right hand touched something hard. Jesus Christ, am I getting hard? He was surprised at the hardness. But he felt warm again. Sure, I'm gonna buy the goddamn house for the kid, even if she's fucking around . . .

"Bob, did ya know my wife's going around with this sonofa*bitch?*"

"Declare!" the Jamaican said when he called the bet.

The air remained tense. Pat looked at Bob and then into the Jamaican's eyes, and slowly he turned over his hole card. "Kings and Aces!" he shouted.

He was laughing with the flag. It wasn't the flag of a king, but what the hell! It was his flag. All his debts were paid.

"Acesandkings!" And his hands moved to the Maple Leafs of bills on the aluminum table. He felt it had been a duel. Over his wife. And he had won.

"Just one motherfucking minute, bredder!" The Jamaican held the long fingernail on his left hand's little finger and eased it under his own hole card. The air was stifling. And when the card was face upwards and Pat saw the three fours exposed and heard the applause and the noise, and Bob assuring and cursing him because, "Pat, didn't ya goddamn see that the goddamn *fourth* four wasn't exposed, even though you had one, and didn't ya remember that the two other Kings was folded in the goddamn pack, in the dead pack, and didn't ya notice that two other Aces was folded in the dead pack, didn't ya notice that, ya stupid bastard?"

Pat saw the Jamaican raking in the bills like leaves at this time of year, as the boys at the track at Woodbine collected discarded tickets, and he could hear the agent's voice on the telephone first thing tomorrow; and he thought he heard even more immediately the voice at the door saying over and over, "Taxi!"; and then all the noise of chairs falling and people running out of his apartment, and the raking of the leaves on the table; and how in a split second the room became quiet, and then moved like jello in his vision, and the Canadian flag which was the only thing he could focus on, and the empty soiled bed sheet. He did not even know when he got up from the table and moved towards the bedroom . . .

CYRIL DABYDEEN

AIN'T GOT NO CASH

There was something odd about Mamie the moment I set eyes on her. I was new to the Bronx; I told her so. Mamie looked curiously at me as fellas in the bar milled around, Puerto Rican types mostly, some black, some white. One fella started calling himself Bongo Santamaria, and everyone laughed. An easy-going atmosphere filled the bar. Mamie said to me, "Maybe you like it here. It's different from Canada, see." The music throbbed, and the fellas swayed their hips. "Yeah, I guess so," I replied in an off-beat way. I was staying with a friend, Miro, for a week. Everyone knew Miro, same as when we were back home (in Guyana). Then, no matter where we went in the district, everyone called out to him, popular as he was. "Hey, Miro, what's up, man?" they'd say. Even complete strangers called out to him. It was the same here in New York I noted. Miro was talking in a back-slapping way with the fella who called himself Bongo. No doubt in this Burnside District, in the heart of the South Bronx, everyone acted in a peculiar way. Well, sort of.

Mamie looked at me, and at once I began to feel different. She drew closer, her heavy-set presence extending from her stool to mine close to the counter. Her eyes seemed larger as she looked at — into — me. Would I agree to her teaching me a Latin dance? she asked. When I didn't reply, she rattled on in an intense way: "Maybe you can get a green card. Yes, you can stay an' work here for a while." She looked ruefully at me, then she turned to Miro, watching him, the muscles bulging along his sleeves, his mouth twitching. Miro was now talking excitedly to a fella in dark glasses, but he seemed aware of us. In a way he was pretending, and I figured he could become an actor if he set his mind to it. Again his mouth twitched, the expression changing — he was now pretending to be angry, then totally happy next as he playfully slapped the fella in dark glasses. Feelings from extreme tenderness to livid rage passed through him in the most extraordinary way.

Miro had been living in the Bronx for the last five years. Why didn't I visit him before, I didn't know. And why I chose to live in Canada instead, I also didn't know. Things just seemed to happen that way, I once said to Miro on the phone. One thing we knew for sure though, we seemed driven away from home. I recalled how Miro and I, as teenagers, often watched re-runs of old American movies. Lots of Humphrey Bogart stuff. Miro, then skinny as an eel, would shout loudly, as if he were mad: "Yeah, I would like to go to America one day, man! I'd love to have all those nice-looking broads for m'self!"

50

Then he was a little like this Bongo fella, who was now slumped in a corner and looking like a zombie. Over the years, however, Miro had fattened, he'd lost a lot of the hair on his head; he looked fierce too when he wasn't laughing. But he was the same Miro, though wily now from time to time, just as when he was in the village. He had an idea up his sleeves each time we talked on the phone. His latest scheme was to start a fire-brand trade union for the part-time patients at the Manhattan Psychiatric State Hospital. "I could raise hell there, man," he declared. He worked from time to time at the hospital. He added, "There are mostly Blacks an' Latins, you know. They need organizing, see. Yeah, that's what I'll do. With a union I'll bust their asses. Even Mayor Ed Koch would take notice, man." But with Miro nothing really ever got off the ground, because the ideas seemed merely to pass in and out of his mind like breeze. No doubt he was telling the fella in the dark glasses, despite the loud music, all about his latest idea. Later he'd tell me also about it.

"He, your friend?" Mamie asked, sensing where my attention was.

"Who?" I asked, as if I didn't know.

"That one."

"Yes." I smiled.

"I've seen him around, you know."

"Oh?"

"Yes. Lots o' times too." Mamie was looking straight at him, boring holes into him with her eyes.

"You could be mistaken. He doesn't come here often." I paused, then added: "That's what he told me."

Mamie seemed to shrink away from me just then. Shortish, she had a thick crop of kinky hair. Her glasses added to the penetrating quality of her eyes, and the way she looked at you the eyes seemed to hold on to you, like clamps. I started telling her of an experience earlier that day when I tried using the public telephone. "There was this dude, you see, mean-looking as hell, who kept hugging the phone to himself for more than an hour. He wouldn't give it up no matter how I tried to get his attention. The phone was like his personal property, you see, so close he kept it, all the while giving me the evil eye. I'd lost my way coming back from Manhattan, and I wanted to get to Miro as quickly as possible."

Mamie casually said New York had a way of doing this to a stranger. It was the first time I was being called a stranger. Then with a flush in her cheeks, she added: "I don't like him."

"The dude?"

"Him. That one — your friend." She pointed, with her eyes.

"Oh?" I was disappointed.

"You shouldn't be staying with him. Heed my warning," she added dryly, Cassandra-like, almost wincing.

"But I've known him for years. We grew up together." I didn't like Mamie saying this. But Mamie, I realized, had a way with words, a way of getting into one's skin. Close by again, she touched me lightly with her large bosom, which I didn't mind. Then something soft about her began to extend to me, though in her eyes there was the usual hardness, the clamps. Mamie asked me my name, because I hadn't told her yet. Everyone called me Sylvio I said. "Okay, Sylvio," she replied, "you like women?"

"What?"

"Women? You like them?"

I shrugged.

"Okay, come on, let's dance. I'll teach you Hispanic moves. You aren't Hispanic, you know. You don't look Hispanic to me."

I decided to play along. We stepped into the middle where everyone else was dancing to loudly throbbing music. We were now only a few feet from Miro, because Mamie really wanted to have a good look at him. Miro was also watching Mamie as she held me closely, tightly, as if I belonged to her. In my ears she said I should move my legs between hers, slowly: it was the way to dance. No need to be miles apart, she chided with a hot breath. "Just listen to the music," she added, "and move your legs, slowly. It's something between a man and a woman, something intimate, private." Suddenly the music was accompanying us, as if Mamie was controlling the musicians. Everyone looked at us.

Mamie added, "You're doing well, Sylvio. Maybe you'll stay in the Bronx forever. Yeah, you'll stay with me, with big Mamie, no?" Her tongue wetted the tip of my left ear, her hot breath in a way tingling me.

I didn't reply, but held her closely and concentrated on the music. The fellow who called himself Bongo now seemed awake, no longer slumped in a corner. She added , "The blacks own this part of town. It's the way it should be. See, I am black too; I don't have to tell you that. Yeah, it don't matter though, black or not."

I didn't know what she was getting at; I merely felt her hot breath against my ears. She seemed to be thinking all the time as we danced. Then she laughed, and once more she looked at Miro, her eyes penetrating, looking through my neck almost, boring holes into my skin. "Say, can you love a woman?" I heard, her thighs fastened between my legs, throbbing, vibrating. What was she getting at? Then the music stopped, as if she also willed this to happen.

"Take me home with you, Sylvio," she said next, urgently, but with a distinct innocence in her voice. The light in the bar dimmed and it seemed we'd been dancing for hours. Smoke swirled everywhere in the room. Watching Mamie, I didn't understand her even though I liked her: something about her heaviness and the way she became easily attached to a guy — to me. She smiled, her teeth showing whitely against sensuous lips.

"Ah, I was just trying you out, you know," she said, almost with guile as she grinned and gulped her drink by the bar. I quickly ordered another for her and kept looking at her.

"Don't get me wrong," she added, "I know lots o' guys, all of them come here too. That Bongo, you see, he's watching me. Yeah, he'll soon leave, but he's still pretending; they're all pretending. It's the way it is in this part of town." She turned and looked at Miro again as if she didn't know what to say or do. Now she grew strangely hesitant.

Bongo began walking out, just as Mamie said he would. Turning to Mamie, I wondered what else she thought; she really fascinated me now.

She continued, slowly, with a distinct drawl: "Yeah, we have a good time in this neighbourhood though, the Blacks an' the Hispanics, we're really one people. But we don't always act like it. Yeah, same roots in slavery, but we don't act like it." She half-scowled, then continued: "Yeah, it's the pretending that gets to me sometimes. Don't get me wrong, I like whites too. My husband, he was honkie. But we couldn't make it together; we were poles apart." She laughed lightly. "It took me three long years to realize that. All the time, you know, he kept insisting he was Hispanic." She turned around once more, looking at Miro; Miro was now coming forward, as if he wanted to warn me about something: that it was one o'clock. He was eager to leave himself since it was so late. But Miro was known to stay out all night drinking.

"Say, aren't you gonna take me home?" Mamie asked.

"Take you home?"

"Yeah." She yawned voluminously. Maybe she too was pretending, her eyes softening as she smiled. I began thinking: Miro wanted me to leave, he wanted Mamie and me to split. Yet I remembered our dance a few moments ago, the way her legs touched mine, the way our bodies vibrated. Then, her fragrance, so wonderful it was, overwhelming me: I was still breathing her. She took my hand across the counter. Suddenly I sensed more of the clamps in her eyes, even in her smile. Her hand squeezed mine, squeezing me into her mass of flesh. Hot flesh, the warmth of her mouth, the roundness and abundance of her face next.

I said I didn't mind taking her home.

Like a warning, Mamie added: "This is a rough neighbourhood, Sylvio. You be careful. Yeah, I like it here though." She continued squeezing my hand, adding slowly, "I teach sometimes too, you know. I thought of teaching regularly, but I never really got round to it. Lots of things need to be done round here. Yeah, lots of work." She looked at Miro. "Him, I don't like," she spat out. Miro was looking directly at her too. In his eyes, he was telling me, urgently, time to go. Mamie said, even as she linked an arm with mine, "I can't stay here much longer. Come on, I don't like him."

"Where are we going, Mamie?"

"To your place," she almost snapped.

"To mine?"

"Yeah," nonchalantly.

I looked at her, a little in awe; I felt I was about to be swallowed by her. Again she began talking about the neighbourhoods; then the music started once more.

Miro started dancing with an attractive, dark-haired woman with huge, sad-looking Hispanic eyes. Their movements were swift, jerky; she followed him along everywhere on the dance floor, swirling, whirling, just for us it seemed. Miro wanted Mamie to look at him, at them. Frustration was everywhere in Miro's manner, his muscles rippling and seeming to extend across the hall to us. Then Miro forgot all about me as he leaned closer to his partner, focussing fully upon her sad face. Now he'd leave me alone with Mamie; a woman often excited him this way. He'd accused me of living too sheltered a life in Canada. Come to America, he urged. He'd been divorced a couple of times.

As his arms and legs extended, Mamie kept being glued to him, even as she continued talking to me about the neighbourhood.

"See," she added, "Blacks have got to learn to respect themselves, to understand each other. I am all for them taking positive action. Self-awareness you know. At one time we tried something here; lots of community work. But nothing seems to change people. Yeah, every outreach program you can think of we tried. Nothing works. Self-awareness is the answer."

But my attention was still fixed on Miro. "Are we leaving?" she asked, abruptly. "Yes, Mamie — no, wait," my thoughts still on Miro.

"Come on, Sylvio, there's no time to waste. Not if you love me." Her eyes widened, like a cow's almost.

The Bronx night air greeted us with drug-pushers, pimps, drunks lingering against door-posts, the night belonging to them. But when Mamie took my arm, she felt as big as the night itself, it belonged to us.

Now she began telling me about a conference she'd organized for unwed mothers. Too many kids, she said, were born in the neighbourhood without knowing who their real fathers were; she wanted to do something about it. She revealed that she herself was born like that. Yet she didn't believe in marriage.

"Yeah," she added, "I don't want to sound like a social worker. I hate social workers. Christ, I much prefer people evolving with their own destinies. It's the way life is." Mamie continued talking in this semi-mystical fashion as we walked on. A Pinto screeched noisily close by and a drunk swore heavily, bringing me back to the present: the night ominous, fearsome.

"Yeah," Mamie went on, my arm still in hers, "it would be easier for the children if they weren't born bastards."

She whirled forward just then; maybe she'd drunken too much. The fellas in the street looked at us with silent, evocative eyes.

Another car screeched in the distance, evoking memories of stray dogs being hit by passing vehicles in the tropical night of my child- hood. My blood raced, brain cells jamming against each other. Someone let out an explosive laugh like gunfire. Mamie also laughed, compulsively, her tongue stretching out as if fanning the night air. She added, "You could stay here all your life, if you want. Yeah, I have a child; I want my child to grow up in this neighbour- hood. Decent, you understand? It's a good place here. You'd like it before long. Ignore the guys, the fellas you see in the dark corners. They only lurk there; it's nothing else for them to do you see. The important thing is to keep loving them."

Mamie was on some kind of a crusade, I thought, and she was mak- ing me a part of it. The air around us whirred with it. She took my arm closer to her as we stepped up the pace, even though Mamie seemed to take her time; time was of no consequence to her.

The key was on the ledge where Miro left it.

Mamie didn't say much now. She merely studied everything I did in a silent, apprehensive way. A large bottle of cheap Italian wine and some Scotch reached out to us from the table, and Mamie poured herself a drink as if this was a perfectly natural act. But she was anx- ious for some reason or the other.

When we kissed, her perfume engulfed me, her breasts almost banging against my chest. Mamie chortled impulsively, then laughed, the sound going across to the next apartment I felt.

It was good that I came to New York, she said. One day maybe, she'd go to Toronto. She thought about it many times, but Canada was really honkie country; the Bronx was her neighbourhood.

"It's part of me, you understand?" she said, smiling, her full lips wet and glistening against the soft light. My face was now buried in her neck as she caressed the back of my head. She said, "You have to learn to love. It's important loving, you see." I fumbled with her clothes.

Mamie added, "It's something between a man and a woman maybe. Time mustn't intervene." She appeared really tense now as she held my hands.

"What's the matter, Mamie?" I asked.

"It's him."

"Who?"

"Your friend —"

"Miro?"

"Yeah."

"What about him?"

"I can hear him."

"Really?"

She nodded.

"You're imagining, Mamie, that's all," I said, my face again in her neck.

"He's close by, just listen. You've got to learn to listen also."

I pretended to listen.

The heaviness of the Bronx night came to me, dim stars in my imagination, the morning slowly raising its head from its curl of sleep. Sun and clouds next: and far, far away, tropical sunshine palpable as jewellery. "Let's get on with it," I said, kissing her again. But Mamie would have none of it; she was too alert, anxious, expecting Miro to burst in at any moment: the same Miro who more than an hour ago danced wildly, being strident and extending everywhere. Well ... Miro was unpredictable. A sound at the door.

It was Miro alright. He said not a word, and walked past us while Mamie remained deathly quiet, her heavy breathing like that of a strangely trapped animal. Miro was taking away something from Mamie, away from the neighbourhood. Suddenly I wished he hadn't come home; I wished too Mamie wasn't acting this way, like a bunched knot or a spring ready to unleash. She whispered, "It's getting late. I should never have come."

From his room, the only one in the apartment, Miro made a heavy sound, letting us know he was still present. Mamie's eyes widened, and she became even more uneasy as she buttoned her blouse. "I must go. Don't keep me here any longer," she kept saying with every act, every expression. "Take me home now — you must," she urged with marked restlessness. The Bronx night was like a bigger spring now. The fellas in the neighbourhood, lurking, their eyes all about, watching for Mamie, me. What did she say? Learn to love them. This was difficult to do, and I became restless too. Mamie's eyes suddenly blazed.

"You must take me home, see. You brought me here," she accused. It was the Bronx expressing itself in her. But, Mamie, I don't dare walk back with you; not out there alone! The night was in me now, making me even more anxious. Was it all because of Miro's presence in the other room? I was a complete stranger, I told her so.

"You're in my neighbourhood," she added firmly.

"It's not safe. New York isn't," I pleaded.

She looked at me incredulously. When she heaved in next, it seemed violence was in her manner, her cheeks rising, then subsiding as she breathed out with a hiss. "You must take me home," she cried softly.

"It's too late, Mamie. Why not stay the night?" I looked at the couch that widened vacantly before us. But simultaneously she cast a glance in the direction of Miro's room. Right then I felt — we both felt — Miro appearing, threatening her as no man perhaps ever did. And I was also saying to her, Miro's part of me; we grew up together, in the same village, the tropics a bond between us. But Mamie remained steadfastly the Bronx, and I was still a stranger.

"Please, you must understand," I said. "You must stay the night."

"I don't trust him, see," she muttered and grimaced simul-

56

taneously. "It's a thing I have, understanding men the way I do."

I took her hand, caressing her once more.

But Mamie was now doing a disappearing act on me: she wasn't with me, she was stiff. Her spirit suddenly a ball of wax. She stiffened further.

"I will not stay. It's your fault, you see, that I came here. Take me home," she pressed.

I fought back, and she expected this. We argued. Finally unable to cope with me any longer — I'd worn her patience — she said, "Okay, give me the money. I'll take a taxi home."

I didn't understand why I hesitated.

Slowly she got up. I figured right then she didn't really want to go, not without me. Her eyes blazed again, then she looked in the direction of Miro's room. Maybe she felt — as much as I did once more — that Miro would burst out upon her. Vaguely she muttered something about her child being without a father. She looked at me again, softly this time, caressing me with her eyes; I felt I was really letting her down, and the entire neighbourhood as well!

"This friend of yours," she said, as if needing to explain something to me, "he doesn't belong here. I know how I feel. It's always been like this with me. I can tell with people right away. Maybe you'll return there. Maybe you don't belong to Canada either." She looked sadly at me. It dawned on me that this was what Mamie wanted to say all along. Why hadn't she said it before?

"You liked her, didn't you?" Miro asked, standing next to me at the door. "The way you were dancing with her, I mean." He convulsed with a quick laugh.

"Yeah," I said, thinking.

"That woman, she's strange. There's many like her here."

"How strange?" I looked accusingly at him.

"Ah," he smiled, towering over me in mock dignified control, his new side intriguing me.

"She said she knew you. She'd seen you many times before," I challenged.

He didn't reply: he was simply savouring the right time to reply. Typical Miro, I thought, the door still ajar, the loud bang somewhere of another door closing in the apartment building, the night still alive. I added, "She's concerned about this neighbourhood, you know. She knows it intimately."

He scoffed. "You're still with her, still in love with her."

I denied this even though as I thought of Mamie, the way we danced, her thighs grazing against mine. The way we touched too, and the soft music, Latin rhythms.

We sat down on the couch to wait for the full light of the morning, like a strange welcoming. "So you're leaving today, back to Canada, eh?" he said.

I'd almost forgotten about it, for I was still thinking of Mamie.

Briefly I saw her in a Toronto street. "Maybe," I said, hoping.

"You wish to stay here longer? The Bronx, a funny place it is. It can grow on you. I don't really know why we came here, why we both left." Nostalgia was written all over him, scarring his face in a way. I thought he wanted to return to his room right then, and sleep during what was left of the night (or morning).

I reminded him that I lived in Canada. He shrugged, he was still reminiscing. Sentimental regret in his voice as he started talking about why we'd left, why we came here, why North America pulled so many of us; something in his tone, our former closeness wedging us again, even as my thoughts continued travelling with Mamie in the taxi . . . and the ones lurking about, watching her, and me.

Miro jolted me by talking about his scheme, the one that had to do with the Manhattan Psychiatric State Hospital. It was at that moment he revealed where he'd first seen Mamie; at the hospital. He grinned. No, he wasn't making this up. It was her alright, and she'd recognized him.

"There's a kind of madness living here, you see: being away from where we came. Yes, it is," he affirmed. He was still sentimental.

While I was still thinking of Mamie. "Why didn't you warn me?" I asked impulsively.

"Warn you?" he seemed surprised.

"Yes."

"With Mamie it's difficult," he replied. "You know, she's changed a lot. That Mamie," his thoughts wandered — "lots of guys around here know her. She likes them all. I don't know though why she doesn't like me." His expression was forlorn, one I hadn't seen in a long time. "Maybe she doesn't trust me."

I waited.

"That Mamie, maybe she trusts no man," he added. "It's always been like that with her. Maybe she'll change. They all do, sooner or later." He paused, before adding, "Yes, I belong here too. Funny how it happens like this. Maybe Mamie could explain it better."

"She really thinks you don't belong here," I said.

"But I do." He raised his voice, looking at me intensely. In his focus I saw Mamie, the two of them as one, and I was the outsider. I looked for the dark-haired Hispanic woman in him as well, beautiful and voluptuous as she was, but I only kept seeing Mamie, the two of them together like clamps. It wasn't just the Bronx now, but something else, hard as this was to explain: something perhaps between them alone, as man and woman, he being what he was, and she being herself. It was in this neighbourhood that they met, evolving their destinies, as Mamie had said.

"Mamie's no doubt at home now," Miro said. "We shouldn't be up like this. You'll be travelling soon. Maybe it's good that she left. Don't worry about her, she's safe. It's her neighbourhood, remember?"

"Not yours?" But my question was muted, for I sensed him being

far apart, the tropics disappearing, and we were now two entirely different persons.

Miro yawned, as he added quickly after: "Yes, it shouldn't be this
way, here in the Bronx I mean. Not in this city at all. In the Big Apple,
you know, people learn to take care of themselves. Maybe one day
you'll see things differently. Maybe you'll even want to come an' live
here. Most people want to at one time or another; then you feel you
belong." He smiled wryly.

I continued thinking about Mamie, her last words about a special
feeling about this place, between a man and a woman; something of
an unexpressed embrace, floated around me, her presence still lingering.

I looked at Miro. Yes, what do you mean? I was asking. He yawned
once more. I figured then I'd see Mamie again, and that she really
trusted me. Unless, I was wrong: and, that in this neighbourhood, it
would always be different, which was what Miro and Mamie were
telling me.

Back in Canada I kept thinking of the pulsation of Mamie's body
as we danced. And when Miro phoned again I saw in him the shutters
of the night, the tropics really far away from us.

MAX DORSINVILLE

BARBARA

We walked back to her place in the student quarter. Posters of Mao and Guevara, flyers of previous marches of the *Third World Committee* were tacked on the walls. She prepared hot chocolate on a portable stove and offered me a cup. She wondered if the march was on the late evening news. Then she sat on the floor, gazed at me, a mysterious smile floating in her eyes.

* * *

Today, years later, she writes to me in Dakar complaining about the snow and envying me. She is bored in Montreal. She still lives in the student quarter but dropped out of the Institute. She spends her time making pottery and hanging around the *Committee*. The comrades and her often talk about their favorite marches. That's when she remembered me. She found out I had resigned from the Institute and left for Dakar. She was living with Gregory, but why should I care she added.

The leper squatted on the doorstep of the post office saw me folding the letter. He mumbled something, his hand stretched out, shaking in the noonday sun. The same words, same movements, every day. To him and the street vendors on Independence Square, I was an American. *Mon frère* . . . who had returned to the ancestral continent, rich. I slipped him fifty francs. An expatriate came up the stairs, eyes unseen behind dark glasses. He steered clear of the leper.
—Any mail?
—A letter.
—Who from?
Denise was used to students dropping by our house in Montreal. She anticipated their visits while doing the weekly groceries. She got into the habit of sharing our lunches and dinners with them since I began teaching at the Institute of African Studies. They were part of our extended family. In Dakar, we kept our distance from the expatriate community. Our chance encounters were brief. They talked about their latest problems with the nannies and the *boys*. They were bored. My research kept me busy at the *Institut Fondamental d'Afrique Noire*. Denise painted. Matthew had his friends at the International School. Sundays at Yoff or Popenguine, Saturdays in Sendaga or Soumbedioune, we basked in the warmth of Africa. We cherished our intimacy, far from our Canadian habits. The car, television, telephone, gadgets no longer summed up our daily life. Loose-limbed, free, we blended with the people on Lamine Gueye, William Ponty or Albert Sarraut, exchanging laughter against the street vendors' calls

60

and *ça va* ... against the nods of men and women gracefully sliding by in their bubus. That Africa, human, alive, swirling in the old and the new, we loved. The other one of the expatriates, with money written all over their faces, we loathed.

—Remember Barbara?

—The Maoist kid ... ?

The tightening of her features let me know that Denise remembered. She finished peeling the potatoes and turned on the burner. The local newspaper lay on the table. I picked up *Le Soleil*. Pictures, endless speeches: the presidential campaign was on. I tried to develop some interest for Abdou Diouf and Leopold Senghor.

* * *

We married in college fifteen years ago. After graduation, Denise worked in a doctor's office. I went to graduate school. Summers, we spent with friends in lakeside cottages. Days spent swimming and fishing under sunny skies. Evenings, beer and wine flowed. We talked endlessly, convinced the world's problems were ours to settle, and that we did. Winters, we got up early and headed for the ski slopes freshly covered with powdered snow. In chairlifts in the early morning fog, we were seduced by the illusion of entering a silent, menacing, snowwhite world. With a Ph.D. in hand, I was offered a post at the Institute. The dye was cast. My life was tied to vast green spaces where in the summertime girls wearing tight jeans kissed barechested boys with long hair.

Early on, my career seemed promising. I befriended my senior colleagues at the Institute. I spared neither signs of respect nor humility. After months of close surveillance, I understood I was accepted in their circle. I knew when to shut up during workshops supposedly held for the benefit of students. Individual vanities reigned. My colleagues' listing of their field work in Africa impressed the students. So they thought. They were "old Africa hands." Africanists they called themselves. They published one or two long articles in journals which no one read. With pages of footnotes longer than the actual texts, these odd articles earned them a reputation of knowledge and expertise on Africa, among themselves. Listening to them, I gravely nodded and frowned with intensity. I had everything to learn. Reassured by my show of respect, they relaxed and told their favorite little anecdotes about life in Lagos, Accra or Dar es Salaam. They all had a sense of humor. They knew their Africans. . . . How they chuckled when memories of native quaintness were exchanged. . . .

One day in the Fall, I sat with my colleagues in a seminar room. The Chairman of the meeting, an anthropologist, introduced the new students. A girl got up. An Africanist said something funny. She smiled. I noticed her dimpled cheeks. Perfect white teeth briefly shined through parted full lips. I saw her next in class, calmly seated, cross legged, a flicker of amused curiosity on her face.

Colonizer, colonized, dispossession, alienation, oppression. . . . I was at it once more. I spotted them quickly, the activists, the sleep-eyed, the stupefied ones reeling under the shock of discovering an Africa other than the stereotypical. As usual, I got excited discussing the theories of Fanon, Memmi, DuBois, Padmore and the rest, tracing pan-African links. I quoted Césaire: the European presence in Africa was part of an imperialist ideology of conquest and exploitation for the sole benefit of Europe. I referred my students to *The Wretched of the Earth* : colonialism had nothing to do with "good" or "bad" settlers. No so-called "good" action justified a master and slave relationship.

Years of practice convinced me my fiery lectures furthered the cause of the decolonization movement. My mission was to keep the movement alive, though far from Africa; the more so as I was struggling against complacency. These obviously well-off boys and girls of the consumer society were to come out of my lectures disturbed and, maybe, feeling guilty. How else once they understood their society's wealth resulted from Third World exploitation? I firmly believed an African sociology course taught at an Institute funded by multinational corporations and administered by a Board of Trustees appointed by these corporations indeed furthered the cause of the decolonization movement. The struggle of Fanon and Guevara would find recruits among the boys and girls of the North American bourgeoisie. My blond, carefree, naive and loving students.

I entered each Fall term with renewed hopes, raising my voice, tightening my arguments, recommending "progressive" readings, emotionally committed to a just and pure cause.

—I like your course. You get straight to the point. No bull shit. The students like that. You're different. It all comes out of books, doesn't it?

The sun filtered in my office that afternoon through half-opened shutters, shafts of light danced on her features. Serene. No movement, no sign of nervousness, none of the usual giggle suggesting that a game was on. She had knocked, then slipped in. Sitting in front of me, her moist lips slightly parted, she gazed at me, totally in control.

—Funny, I bet you're playing a game. You talk a lot. I've been watching you. You know it. It bugs you.

—Interested in psychoanalysis?

—Relax. You know what I mean.

—I don't. . . . I don't have time for guessing games.

—. . .

Her eyes glowed mischievously. The whiteness of her teeth shined. She nodded sharply, businesslike.

—I didn't come here to get inside your head. Psychoanalysis bores me. There's a demonstration tonight. You saw the posters on campus? I'm on the organizing committee. We'd like to have you with us. We'll start from the Community Centre on St. Urbain. You're coming?

—What demonstration?

—On behalf of the Haitian refugees. They'll all get killed if they're sent back to Haiti.

I lit up a cigarette, breathed in deeply and blew the smoke out, leisurely fashion. Her eyes were riveted on me, anticipating my next move.

—You know . . . these street activities, marches, as you call them, I leave that to students. I used to believe in that sort of thing when I was your age. Why don't you run an open letter in the papers? Circulate a petition, get well-known names to sign. . . .

I was scrambling to "establish distance," as my colleagues said when they were called upon.

She broke up laughing.

—And this from the man who gets all choked up in class talking about oppression and exploitation? Come on, man, let others play the bull shit game. There are Blacks, yeah Blacks like those you talk about in class . . . right here in Montreal, their lives are at stake. The fathers of your students are their judges. Are you gonna let them destroy these poor people and sit on your ass doing nothing?

She got up, scraping the floor with her chair, breathing heavily.

—Listen . . .

She stopped. Her face softened. Her whole body seemed to melt as she sat down, her chin propped up in her hands, her arms resting on her knees.

—What's your game?

She seemed startled. Her eyelids moved rapidly, she sank further in the chair and crossed her arms. Her jaws hardened menacingly. Her face became an inscrutable mask, her brown eyes, dilated, froze in a fixed expression.

—All right, I'll come along.

She smiled.

* * *

—I was born in Kenya. Lived there eighteen years. My parents were missionaries, still are. I finished High School in Nairobi two years ago, then came here. See that picture. That's me when I was three, and that's my nanny. A Kikuyu. I wonder where she is now. I loved her. She taught me to speak. My mother tongue is Kikuyu. Funnyeh? My parents didn't teach the Bible only. They took care of the sick and did all kind of work in the village. They built the first hospital and the first school in Kassa. That's the name of our village. At first, we had no electricity. My father had a generator sent in from Canada by the Brethren of the Assembly of God. I remember the evenings we'd spend out on the veranda. I'd sit next to my father and we'd look at the villagers squatted in the yard around a brazier. They'd softly sing their traditional songs and they'd tell tales of the forest. We'd join them and exchange charades. I lived in the village until I was twelve.

we were one great big family. See those bangles? They were given to me by my nanny. As long as I wear them, she told me, I'd return to Massa. I never take them off. . . .

She stopped talking and shook her wrists. She listened to the jingle of the copper bangles, fascinated.

The march had ended in front of the Immigration Appeal Board building in Old Montreal. One of her comrades offered us a lift. She preferred walking. We came up St. Lawrence and turned on Milton, talking all the way, excited. Her hands deep in her coat pockets, she kept a brisk pace. We bumped against each other, on purpose it seemed. On Lorne Avenue, she asked me to come in.

Posters of the revolutionary left faced me in the room where she ate, studied, cooked and talked to her friends. There was a printed cloth of Mount Kilimanjaro over a small bookshelf. Next to a Bible and a Swahili-English dictionary, some paperback editions of Marx, Engels, Lenin and Mao. Two framed pictures caught my eye. One was of a man about fifty years old with a piercing look behind heavy-rimmed glasses, straight jet black hair flat on the skull, an authoritarian mouth topped by a no-nonsense mustache. The other showed a woman about sixty, white hair pulled back in a bun, the tired but satisfied look of one who knew she was doing God's duty. Her parents.

* * *

—It's in High School I began to understand. I was White in a Black society. My friends were Americans, British, Canadians and other Whites living in Kenya. There wasn't a single Black student in the school all the time I was there. Except in my senior year when they admitted three under pressure. The government threatened to cut off the school's grants. Our teachers were White, of course. That was colonial life, all right. I didn't understand that at the time. Anyway, I shared in all the privileges of being White in Africa. I'll never forget that. Even to this day, I don't understand why my parents sent me to that school. Sometimes I'd go home during the holidays. It had changed. Some childhood friends were still in the school my father founded. They were learning farming. They really wanted to study mechanics. Those who left the village occasionally came back. They worked in garages in Nairobi. They wore loud clothes, dressed to kill. Tight-fitting pants, caps down to their ears, eyes hidden behind dark glasses night and day. In gangs, they passed in front of our home and would point to it sniggering, elbowing each other. I'd go out and walk up to them. They'd turn their heads and pretend they didn't know me. So I stayed with my High School friends. I'd go to Mombassa for sailing and deep sea diving. My friends lived in beautiful villas. Houseboys in white jackets, silent and obedient, were on beck and call. I had a boyfriend, more than one actually, but that one was special. His father was the manager of the Chase Manhattan Bank. He was tall, blond, freckle-faced. Ted was his name. He wanted to get married. I was seventeen, can you imagine! He was twenty-one. He was going to Harvard in the Fall. He left by himself. I got a scholarship from the Assembly of God. My parents were happy. They were getting worried with each passing year I spent in Africa. They sought the Brethren's help to get me out. They said they wanted me to find my roots in the southwest of Ontario they called *home*. Once the registration papers came through I left for boarding school in Canada. I didn't stay long. I'll tell you some other time. . . .

* * *

I wonder if Barbara still wears her bangles.

MADELINE COOPSAMMY

THE TICK-TICK BICYCLE

Every night after supper, Sharon heard it. Tick, tick, and the lights would flash, like those of a circus horse. She would see him, leaning backwards on his bicycle, grinning sardonically, and looking into their front porch. In spite of the semi-darkness of the porch, the street light would reveal, to her frightened eyes, his form elevated to a mysterious strength and power by the shining glory of the bicycle. She had seen him when he was not astride his flashy machine in its souped-up beauty, how ordinary and insignificant he was. But when he rode through the streets of San Juan de la Pina on his tick-tick bicycle, he owned the world.

She began to dread going out on the porch after supper. Yet to remain inside the house where the tropical heat saturated her body and seemed to addle her mind would be to admit her guilt. She would wait until she thought it was safe to come out. But often she miscalculated his hour, or he had returned, not having seen her the first time. After he had gone, she found it difficult to concentrate on her studies, and too often she could not fall asleep. Sometimes, long after everyone was sleeping, she was sure that she heard it again. Tick, tick, and through the fine weave of the lace curtain, she thought she saw the flash of lights as his bike went by. She would get up and make sure that the window was shut tight, though the heat would almost suffocate her.

They called him Wild Bill Hickok, most often, Wild Bill. The Caribbean island of Trinidad, in the 1950s, was by no means the plains and mountains of the American Wild West. But Trinidad youths, for a few cents, could relieve the tedium of their lives by absorbing the celluloid fantasies of Hollywood. And so it became easy for them to adopt the names of its heroes and vagabonds, no matter how incongruous. Wild Bill was known to all the residents of San Juan de la Pina, an amorphous part of the town that could not be classified as a suburb but was not completely part of the business world.

The district of San Juan de la Pina was bound by two parallel arteries, each the opposite of the other. On one side was the Northern Main Road, bustling with commerce, traffic and bacchanalian revelry every night of the week. On the other was the softly residential avenue known as Cumana. Several nondescript but divergent streets linked these two passageways. But wild Bill made himself equally at home on his tick-tick bicycle as he veered casually between the two territories. Everyone knew him, accepted him as part of the landscape, as just another idler, another young man who lounged about the clubs and cafes, or "parlours" as they were called, of the Main Road. How he lived, no one knew or cared. Wasn't it enough that he owned a tick-tick bicycle, the most flamboyant of its kind? But to Sharon, consumed by fear of him, hating him for the chaos he was wreaking on her hitherto peaceful life, he was more than an idler. She had heard it whispered that he was dangerous. But why exactly, no one dared to say.

And so, she had always kept her head high when she passed him on the Main Road, as he slouched against a post or leaned against his bicycle; and even though he always muttered sly remarks under his breath, or whistled at her, she never looked at him as she had been warned. She treated him as any other wastrel. But that was before. Now it was different. In the past, he had appeared and disappeared at irregular intervals. Now he was always around. She began to fear walking on the Main Road alone. But most of all, she dreaded the hour after supper when he would be sure to ride by, the tick-tick of his bicycle echoing every fearful beat of her own heart.

Perhaps, if he were not the proud owner of such a status symbol as a tick-tick bicycle, she could dismiss him as of no consequence. But because of the bicycle, he considered himself King of the Main Road, where all the unemployed and unschooled young men congregated, doing odd jobs, or shooting pool in the beer parlours. When he was not standing on the cornber of the Main Road, sniggering at the girls, he was seen crouched over the low handlebars of the ten-speed bicycle, which was shinier, newer, boasted more lights and more gadgets than that of any other youth. Above all, it seemed to have the loudest, most persistent tick-tick in the area. What he had added to the bike to create that sound, Sharon never knew.

When Sharon and her mother were returning from visiting relatives, many blocks away, they saw him, hanging backwards on his bicycle, grinning at them. Her mother had cautioned her not to show any fear, saying sternly, "He's only one of those no-good idlers. Besides, he's a big coward, everyone knows that. He'll never molest us."

If you had said that a few months ago, Mother, you might have been right, Sharon thought. But now, it's different. And she trembled when he passed by. Still, she dared not say anything to her mother. For her mother would only worry, as she always did. Sharon was old enough to know that life was not easy for her mother, having to bring up five daughters by herself, while her husband worked in Venezuela, "in the oil fields" as people in Trinidad always described it. Sharon had heard that expression so often in her childhood that she had imagined the neighbouring country as one huge field of oil, and its landscape broken only by enormous derricks. As she grew older, she became more accustomed to the reality of a father absent most of the time. on his trips home, she learnt to make fine distinctions about the country in which her father spent most of the year. She began to understand that Maracaibo was different from Caracas and that Latin Venezuela, though only eleven miles away, had little affinity with British Trinidad. But her father's twice a year visits were never enough. When she complained, her mother explained that this was the only way in which they could be brought up in the style to which they were accustomed. "Times are hard now," her mother said, "and people like us are not like common people. But because she had no brothers, and because her father was never there, Sharon felt that they had no one, no strong man to protect them from Wild Bill.

She never told her mother: how could she bring herself to explain that Wild Bill had taken to riding past their house more regularly now than before, and that she — and no common girl of the street — was responsible for this? That he was pedalling his tick-tick bicycle up and down their quiet, respectable street, because of her and not because he was waiting for some servant girl from one of the neighbouring houses? That if it hadn't been for her, he would now be hanging around on the Main Road rather than disturbing her serenity by the nagging tick-tick of his bicycle down their street every night? If only she had not been so self-willed. She shivered whenever she heard the sinister sound of the bicycle. In the daytime, when she took the bus to go to school in the town, she felt safe from him. It was too early for him to be about, idler as he was.

But in the afternoons, after school, she could never bring herself to go to any of the stores on the Main Road, even though it was necessary to do so. Perhaps she had to buy some lace or ribbon for her sewing class the next day, or else incur the wrath of Sister Veronique, the sewing teacher. Now, however, she would have to wait until one of her sisters could go with her, for he would be sure to be there, not sitting or standing, but half-leaning against a pillar, or his bicycle. Often, Sharon wondered why it was that Wild Bill managed to convey the impression of evil, even though he was, in reality, quite nice-looking. He was never drunk, nor did he ever smell of rum. He was always well-dressed, in the jeans and wide belts that were becoming fashionable in Trinidad at that time. But whenever Sharon looked directly into his eyes, their smallness never ceased to amaze her. There was something strange about them, she would think. And why did he have to straighten his hair, instead of letting it curl in its natural way? Surely that was the mark of an idle young man's vanity. Everyone had come to expect Negro women to straighten their hair with a hot comb and lots of brilliantine. All modern Negroes did it, instead of plaiting their hair in the corn-row style of their African cousins. But sensible people could not abide seeing such straightening in a man's hair. Respectable old men never indulged in such vanity. But the "Hot Boys" of the town, as they were called, those frequenters of the "Pit" section of the cinema, were the ones who sported such a fashion. But Sharon had to admit that the eyes, the straightened hair — they

68

were of no real consequence. It was the mouth, the cynical, sneering mouth, the lecherous grin that never ceased to dismay her.

Although she was sure everyone in her family knew of her fear, and that they hated her for the disgrace she was going to bring upon them, she could never bring herself to talk about Wild Bill. She was too ashamed of her weakness and bad judgement and of how she had pestered her mother to go to the Allens' party that night three months ago. Her arguments with her mother had been long and bitter.

"But everyone — all my friends in class — are going, Mother. Why I alone must stay home every Friday night? I never get to go to *fetes* like everyone else."

"You can go to *fetes*, yes," her mother would counter, "but *fetes* in decent places, to nice people's homes, not with people like that."

"But the Allens are decent people, Mother. They come to Church every Sunday."

"You are too young to understand, girl. You will be sorry later on in life. I don't want you going out with any and everybody. Remember who your grandfather and uncles are."

"So my grandfather is a white man, and my uncles are doctors. But my father is a brown man and we live in this rat-hole and pretend that we're better than everybody else. Well, I don't want to pretend any more. I want a normal life."

Her mother's face had taken on that veil of fear and hurt over it that always frightened Sharon. This always had the effect of making her back off from any further confrontation with her mother. Mrs. Damien was a thin, nervous woman who sometimes retreated into her own fantasy world when life's realities became too much for her. Always fearful of her mother's precarious hold on the world, Sharon had resigned herself to not going. But then Mrs. Damien had suddenly announced, "I asked Aunt Margie if I should let you go to the Allens' *fete*, and she said it should be okay."

Surprised, Sharon had nothing to say, but one thought was uppermost in her mind. You asked Aunt Margie, a worse snob than yourself? And she said yes? Aunt Margie? That is real strange. It suddenly came to her that the Allens were relatively well-off. Aunt Margie usually rated people according to how "high-coloured" they were; that is, according to how much white blood they showed. Could it be that the old biddy felt that the Allens' money made up for their lack of "high colour"? Sharon decided that it was too complex to worry about. She could already hear the steel band music pounding in her ears and feel the capypso rhythms in her body. She could see her classmates' laughing faces. And she knew which boys would be there too, but it didn't matter, for the Allens' second boy would be there for sure. And she couldn't wait to talk to him again. He was so intelligent, his eyes behind his horn-rimmed glasses were so deep and kind.

And then Wild Bill had to spoil it all — by crashing the party. And no one, none of the adults or young men there had cared enough to throw him out. And though everyone was having a good time, she felt that many of them looked as if they had had too much to drink. She found it strange that there were so many adults. She could not imagine her mother or any of her aunts at this kind of party, so relaxed and comfortable, and laughing and teasing the teenagers. Now at last she had a glimpse of another Trinidad, the Trinidad of the "common people" from which her mother and her aunts shielded her so well.

And when Wild Bill had come in, he had walked straight up to her. It was as if he had sensed that she was easy prey. And her fear of offending, her desire to be liked by these people, even though they were people that her mother might call common, was uppermost in her mind. Wild Bill had stood in front of her and asked her for a dance! For a few seconds, which seemed like hours, Sharon just sat there, unable to either refuse or accept. But her inexperience, her self-consciousness and sensitivity, made her feel as if everyone waited with bated breath to see what she would do — for Sharon was aware, from the moment she walked into the room — that she was the only one of her kind there. Her skin was white, that pasty white of thin Trinidad, and her hair showed traces of negro blood visible only to the sharp-eyed who looked for such things. Perhaps everyone there would think that she was snubbing Wild Bill because she felt superior to them all.

And so she got up. Got up to dance with Wild Bill! If her mother or any of her sisters were to see her, she knew that she would die of shame. But they weren't there, and she tried to hold herself stiffly, and prayed that the dance would soon be over. But he wouldn't let her. He clutched her suffocatingly close to himself. She cringed, inside herself. But outside, she was dancing around the floor with him, and she felt every eye in the room riveted on them, every voice censoring her. But what could she have done? She was not experienced enough to know that Wild Bill would never have been an invited guest, that in spite of the happily-intoxicated older people, it was still a "decent" party. The youngsters there were all high school students, a privileged class. They were far removed from someone like Wild Bill, idler, lounger-at-large, and unemployed in spite of his tick-tick bicycle and its flashing lights.

In her reflective moments, when she tried to convince herself that Wild Bill would not dare to harm her, she replayed in her mind's eye the scene of that night, what she had done, how she had acted, and how she had looked. Then she was convinced that it had been her fault. For again Wild Bill had come back and asked her to dance. And having danced once, how could she refuse? And the third time. But then, the Allens' second boy who had been sitting next to her and talking about *The Aeneid* and Vergil, had suddenly got up and said to Wild Bill, "Sorry, boy, she's dancing this one with me." And she had been saved. Wild Bill had never come back and asked here to dance again, contenting himself with ogling her in a slimy way from across the room. But Sharon felt dirtied, almost as if she should go to Confession. Or as if she had broken one of the most sacred rules of the Convent, and that the Nuns would soon be asking her to leave, the ultimate disgrace that could befall a Convent girl. For she was no good, she associated with Wild Bill hickok, anathema to all they hold dear.

Sometimes when she couldn't sleep at night, she thought about how the characters in books and movies would get away from people like Wild Bill, and she often thought that the easiest would be to "fall under" a car. At other times she was sure that he would come to her house that night, perhaps when she was asleep, and he would break open the window. What would be even worse, he would park his tick-tick bicycle in front of her house and walk up their front steps during the hour after supper when her whole family was sitting on the porch. And he would walk up the steps and stand on their porch just as if her were any of the "decent" boys that came to visit. Then her mother and sisters would find out, and they would be hurt and embarassed. They would blame her for bringing this shame upon them, this association with the lowest of the low, with this toad that idled his life away on street corners calling out names to the girls as they passed by.

A day passed by and she saw no sign of him. Then another day. After a week had gone by and he still had not appeared, she hoped and prayed that he had moved away and that she would never see him again. Or that by the time her returned, she would be grown-up, with a boy-friend or husband so big and strong that Wild Bill would not dare to trouble her any more. Or that she might have left the island, "gone away" as most young people did when they finished high school. Then one day a headline in the newspaper caught her eye:

WILD BILL SENTENCED TO FIVE YEARS

William A. Carter, also known as Wild Bill Hickok, of no fixed place of address, was yesterday sentenced to five years in the Royal Gaol for breaking and entering. Carter, who had a record of previous offences, had been convicted before on charges of "peeping Tim" behaviour and of molestation of females.

An earlier charge against Carter, that of statutory rape, had been dropped. In sentencing Carter, the Judge made it clear that he would have been more lenient with him, if only he could have ascertained that Carter, at any time in his life, had held down a steady job. "Instead," the Judge continued, "the evidence of the Court proved that you spend your hours on street corners, badgering females, and scrounging a meal from anyone you can find. And so," added the Judge, "I feel compelled to put you away for five years."

GERARD ETIENNE

DEAF WOMAN

(Excerpt from a novel)

CHAPTER ONE: CRISIS

It is 6 a.m. Marie-Anne's eyes are still open. She has just spent another sleepless night in a room, head over heels, where her Negro barricaded her four days ago. Suddenly she jumps off the bed and stands in front of the mirror of her dressing table. She looks at herself for a long time, utterly aghast, horrified by the zombie's reflection that she has become in such a short time. She squats flat against the piece of furniture and feels her bony cheeks where wrinkles are beginning to show. She starts to moan. She falls flat on her face on the carpet. She trembles, utters the heart-rending cry of the possessed. She punches her belly. She writhes about as if she has a fish in her bowels. In order to give more weight to her rage and fight against the feeling of helplessness, she rips off her negligé and bites at her wrist until blood comes out.

She has now reached the limit of her endurance. Images of death have torn her mind so that her head has become the enemy of her body. Days have passed since she was manhandled in her room, then locked in. Since then, she rummages in what she has left of her memory to look for the moment when she ceased to be considered as the godsend woman, but as a flunkey relegated to a room in a house in Outremont. Half an hour after her confinement, she thought that her husband's anger was momentary as he was tired of his wife's sulking. But Gros Zo's contemptuous attitude since he received his L.M.C.C. diploma, the rope attached to the window sill, the bewitched doll placed under her pillow, as well as the coconut with two death's heads on each extremity, her slashed wedding picture, all these things indicate that she will not come out alive from her cell, that the voodoo spirits called upon by the doctor in his office on his return trip to Haiti are markings on the walls of her room.

Marie-Anne realizes that she is not dreaming any more. The more she loses her strength, the more she notices that Gros Zo's bad spirits are putting a finishing touch on their assault, as he had seen them prowling about her in her nightmare last Wednesday. They were swelling in their double-breasted coats, making their ram's horns move. Their wings bumped against the ceiling and raised her jewellery boxes that knocked against each other. Their legs gave the tempo to the voodoo dances which attracted other satans greedy for blood.

What was to upset her, though, was the thunder going with Gros Zo's spirit's laughter. It was making the house tremble, the trees outside tremble.

The young woman's shrieks seem to tire her out. She remains lying flat on her face, as if to protect herself against the machine-gun burst directed at her chest. The bell sounds for the first time. Then a second time. She holds back a scream in her throat so as not to attract attention. She is more and more convinced of her nearing death. After all, better to die in that house, great as her anguish is, than in the mud morass where her man wants to submerge her. For Marie-Anne, it will be a long agony, because she has thrust herself into the thick night with moans that belong to a defeated woman. Now her eyelids are swollen under the salt of her tears.

In Joyce Park, the cries of the last birds of summer sound sorrowful because of the autumn's first cold. It's as if in one single blow, the great breath of the green spaces in the neighbourhood in Outremont has taken the shape of an ice-box in which the poor corner of the tropical sky will be caught. It seems that this neighbourhood perched on a hill will soon close itself in a silence that will be broken only by the rumblings of the tank trucks.

Marie-Anne does not know how to free herself from the webs of images that are torturing her. To complete her misfortune, she realizes that her tongue is becoming paralyzed as her fever increases, as her body breaks up like a seashell thrown into a vat full of acid. She makes a last effort to regain her reason, the image of the revolutionary woman she was in high school before ending up in an adventure for which the end is reformatory school. Then she pirouettes in her illness. She wants to catch up in her sunray, with that earth scent coming in through the window once the drops of dew in the grass of her garden have disappeared.

She starts to go around the room. She stops every five minutes in front of a wardrobe, smells from afar the shirt Gros Zo was wearing the day he let out before her face his contempt for the negress. She tries to relax, to convince herself her husband will finally open the door. To no avail. Her temples are beating heavily. It feels as if her head is going to burst, that she is on the edge of madness; nothing will stop the doctor's vengeance. The males of her country suffer a kind of illness which takes the form of ill-place pride or the expression of cowardice negating the years of hardship and misery of the negress so as to help them reach the top of society. She is more or less conscious of the havoc caused by that illness. It will have caused many deaths. Ten, twenty thousands of women maybe, in that same city, with their minds eaten by vermin, completely scattered by germs of that vengeance. Or somewhere else. And mostly there, in her country made of the deaths and the mud. Of stinking bloody furrows. That country similar to her face. Flaccid. Heavy.

Marie-Anne is losing her blood more and more. She fights herself, against her weakness. Rejected by her ancestry, she sees herself move within a circle populated by demons. By sharks. However, at the very time angels' voices render her mute, her mother's picture, the rebellious negress who had the reputation of being a demon in their village, stirs up her strength. Then she starts to cry again. Her muscles swell at once. Then armed with the strength that comes from being at the tip of despair, she begins to dismantle the door of her room. She is successful.

Leaping into the corridor of the second floor of the house, she looks at Gros Zo's portrait hanging from the wall of the stairway with hate. The idea that she may die violently gives her a feeling of pride. Gathering all her courage, she blows up the first barrier. Then a second one. Finally, she is able to kick the front door of the castle open. On the sidewalk, she stands blinded by daylight. She closes her eyes in order to appreciate fully the morning scent that seemed, a moment ago, to stand still in her madness. She lets out, with all her might, the scream of an animal that has been hurt, of a slave that has been whipped to death but who refuses to beg for mercy.

The sky slowly hides itself from her, like a liquid image hard to immobilize on the canvas. As she thought herself liberated from the hold Gros Zo's evil spirited objects had on her, terrifying images obstructed her eyes. Gangs of Shrove Tuesday following the rhythm of the tom-toms rumbling on the streets surround her as if to prohibit her from moving. They utter muffled moans similar to the sea's noise, to the moans of the scum of society where starved bellies fold upon themselves so as to escape the anguish of not having anything to eat. In those gangs eaten by fever, she notices ill-treated negresses, powdered, not anguished but laughing, eating up the dust of a dirty afternoon. It is the same undulation of the waist similar to the whirlwind in the hot night of a hurt cricket.

Nailed to the sidewalk, the young woman is unable, as she just escaped from the power from the power of evil spirits in her room, to disengage herself from the beast's claw. She keeps on seeing it tumbling in front of her, with an open mouth, with a bent back, its paws hitting the ground. And while that beast raises itself at the height of a bank of steam surrounding Joyce Park, sounds of lambi are heard. She feels that all is collapsing. Soon, only hot cinders will remain under her feet, portrait of a young woman having completely lost her mind.

Marie-Anne tries to stare at the sun. The breeze dies at her feet. Strange creatures keep on giving her the once-over, as if she was a piece of merchandise, that black madonna on whom drifts the desire of the young man at the threshhold of adolescence. Rising to the surface of dizziness, she realizes that she is upsetting the peace of the neighbourhood as she is tucking her negligé up to her chin. More she attempts to reason with herself, though, more she feels like going to the bottom of her derangement, to precipitate her fall, because she will have to assume the hurt she gave herself while accepting satan's claws in all the pores of her skin. She would like to remain a long time in that state. Because she believes that good manners, good education prohibit the negress from spitting on her male's shit, from defying a hypocritical society which pampers the strong man while accepting his litanies on the subject of freedom.

At the corner of Hartland and Kelvin streets, Marie-Anne embraces a tree. The cold bites her ears and her fingers rebellious to the seasons' metamorphosis. Her weakened voice barely utters grunts of pain. Around her, a humming group of children is going to school. She massages her belly. A cramp causes her to bite her tongue. Ghosts' arms strain towards her in order to wrest from her her tormentor's hate. She thinks that it would be so easy if those devils would have pity on her, that feeling that is unknown to the evil people of her land, that kind of bliss in the soul, bliss that does not question the pain one feels when one sees an old man lying in frozen mud.

Morning slowly recedes in front of the smell of the wet pavement. The lukewarm autumn sun projects long forms that seem to scramble on brick walls at regular intervals. Steam in the form of lead soldiers dances on the roofs of houses. For the time being, only the far away noise of a bus accompanies the fall of the leaves. A man, in his thirties, staggers. The neighbourhood's scenery seems to give out a gloomy atmosphere magnified progressively by the noise made by scrap-iron that makes the earth's flesh shudder. Lajoie Avenue extends to infinity, leaving the walker with the mysterious sensation that the following night will make even more subtle.

Marie-Anne succeeds in making her legs move. She clenches her teeth. Starts to limp on. She goes around Joyce Park for a first time. Then, she goes round each electric pole like a ribbon braider. She wants to do something in order to appease that racket that is burning all parts of her body. Finding again her negress agility, she contracts her muscles, and starts running in the park. She runs forward, backward, around. She looks desperately for a certain liberation inside her derangement in the space that embraces her.

She leaves the park. She stumbles while going up Kelvin Street. Goes down Dunlop Street while pulling up a few shrubs along the sidewalk. She stops at the end of the street, but starts again after a few seconds. She enters again the courtyard of the Holy-Name-of-Mary boarding school. Goes round each tree. Then the building. As if she wanted to find, in that religious place, some answer to her harrowing metaphysics, or to take the portrait of the Virgin Mary, the one that is placed as an effigy on voodoo altars of Haiti, and jealously hidden in Gros Zo's instrument-case.

Marie-Anne is running faster. Her half-torn negligée becomes inflated because of the wind. From everywhere in the neighbour-hood, sounds reach her, urging her to run faster in order to arrive at her very quick, making her jump over the distance separating her state of crushed negress from the woman able to assume her madness to the point of splitting herself in order to master her weakness. She is running. Her braids jump on her forehead. She swallows one or two puffs of air in front of the town hall. She goes along McEachern Street, goes again up Lajoie Street till she reaches Joyce Park where she stops, breathless, exhausted. She lies down on a bench and goes to sleep.

Marie-Anne slowly opens her eyes. She dribbles at the corner of her lips. Pain lines her face. Cramps in her belly make her moan. She is dead. Tangled in a web of strings which bind her to a machine that explores every recess of her skull. She feels that they want to dismantle her brain in order to find the kind of tropical parasite that is responsible for her being unhinged this autumn morning. The young woman looks at the machine. She does not stop bawling around her head. Controlling her mechanical moves. Her bogey teeth. Invisible hands manipulate the motor in the dead woman's body. Without speaking of the tubes that bring the salted taste of disinfectant and rubber to the patient's lips.

The young woman is sure that the machine has broken something in her while she was unconscious. Her mind, in confusion, has not measured yet the distance one has to cross in order to occupy a territory where whe will control her body. While forcing herself to go over her imprisonment, in her own house, she wants to convince herself that she is not the first one to aggress her male's space, or to fall in such a state of misconduct as to chance to see an army of well-meaning people revolt against her. She tries moving. Her feet, her chest, and her hands remain immobile in a straight jacket. Then, Gros Zo was not wrong. He had called her a beast and a slave. Without identity. He had said: "Negresses like her can only submit to the will of the master." That goes up in her throat. Because, by debasing her, one forces her at the same time to hide like the beast in an environment made of rubbish.

She believes, however, that she will have to break through the ice over her head. She will have to muffle the protesting voices each time a woman prisoner tries to break adrift. To go to the depth of her madness, with its own logic, with its reduced corridor, without waiting for the sunset over the mountain in order to find a reason to howl out for life.

On the fifth floor of the La Fontaine building, the day will be long. Two patients have already tried to force the doors of their cells. Another one has just scratched a doctor's face. Tears are raining in La Fontaine building. Cries. Solitude. Anguish too. In their straight jackets, patients are murdering their images. They scream loudly. The echo of their voices is making the building rock. They scratch, they bite by way of replying to pity, to morality.

Marie-Anne breathes slowly. A Haitian doctor enters her cell that is lit by a yellowish light. He looks strict, like an all-powerful man

76

standing in front of a lined group of nurses. Through her eyelids, numbed with morphine, Marie-Anne recognizes Doctor Hippolyte; he has already spent his anger on the black woman; he would be the one who set Gros Zo against the presence of a negress in such a beautiful house in Outremont. Then, she moves convulsively in her straight-jacket. Because she never thought that the first human face she would confront would be the one of an enemy. Already he looks at her with contempt, like a punch in the eye, a hot iron on the flesh that makes you jump like a stamped beast, or an electric discharge in the middle of the spine.

Marie-Anne is barely able to hold her anger in check. The smallest mistake would be sufficient to sign her death sentence. She closes her eyes in order not to see her tormentor's ugly face, so as not to give him the certainty of being his victim, the submitted woman represented by Marie-Thérèse who was ordered locked up by him last year because of a migraine. She pretends to sleep in order to better see as images the portrait of the one on whom her husband's redemption, the freedom of all men of his kind, guilty of the downfall of thousands of Haitian women depend. She has seen enough in a downtown jail, a real market where wild odors were competing with the desires of the male. Before her breakdown, she had seen one of Doctor Hippolyte's victims sitting in a corridor, strangled, besides herself, beyond time. For a few seconds, all those women remain clinging to Marie-Anne's mind, to the point that she feels herself slipping in the same depth, in the same volcano where the weight of their social class is strangling them.

Doctor Hippolyte bends over Marie-Anne. His look is so scornful that the head nurse decides to step back so as not to be an accomplice. He scrutinizes her as if she were already a package of decomposing meat that Gros Zo's devils would have left to science after having plucked out her soul. She pretends to be dead. She keeps her body stiff. Her paralysed tongue does not succeed in speaking works that express the hatred and scorn that this hypocritical doctor inspires in her. She would spit them out if only some power could unblock the mechanism which makes the mouth's muscles work. They would have been vulgar words going through the body like barbs. Which would return everywhere. In the ears as in the nose. In the rooms as in the books of those who fight for justice. Words to spit out the truth, then and there, in cell 580, La Fontaine block. Words to tell the nurse who wiped her face with such friendship when she regained consciousness that this serious Haitian doctor is only his gorilla's accomplice. He would have left her to rot in a room just to get rid of a negress who bothers him in his relations with high society people. He has given himself all the power, even to the point of deciding that his wife is mad, and that she has to be locked away.

Doubtlessly embarrassed by the way the head nurse looks at him, intrigued by his arrogant attitude with the patient, the doctor begins to act like a good samaritan. He swallows his saliva, and with an ironical tone says to the young woman: "We need your collaboration, Madame. You will tell us everything, won't you?"

Marie-Anne moves her tongue; she would like to find some saliva to spit at the doctor's face; the hypocrite pretends not to recognize the wife of a colleague, a fellow countryman working in this same hospital. Unfortunately her throat is dry. She controls her breathing during the doctor's interrogation. Faced with the young woman's indifference, the healer's voice becomes more serious. His tone rises.

"You must tell us everything, Madame. Are there any mad people in your family? How did it occur? As very often happens in your country, did you sign a pact with forces of the occult, or did you lose your head during a vodoo ceremony?"

Marie-Anne makes one last effort to articulate a few words. She doesn't succeed. It's a fact, she has lost the power of speech. Filled with disgust, she turns away her head.

The doctor gives a long speech to the intern and nurses. Among other things, he denounces Canada's policy which favours the immigration of this class of Haitian women; the contact with a technologically advanced milieu makes them crazy. He takes this woman as an example. "She doesn't even understand French," he says. The West Indian doctors, according to him, have difficulty in communicating with these stupid women. According to the doctor, the Minister of Immigration should hire translators capable of describing the demented world of these West Indians. He once again leans over Marie-Anne: "My dear, you don't have any faith in science; you would like to see a voodoo doctor in my place. Perhaps you are truly possessed by a demon? But know this, Madame. In the first place, the voodoo gods do not cross the ocean. They only have power in Haiti. Secondly, voodoo has never cured tuberculosis nor heart disease. Here we can reconstruct your mind."

It's as if a poisoned arrow has entered Marie-Anne's flesh, a clap of thunder causing her brain to explode, this allusion to the spirits that she has so much difficulty to get rid of. Then the room starts to spin around her. Under her bed, she feels an angry sea, a pile of ashes where the dragon who has come to behead her is moving. People come around the dead body that she believes she has become. On the doctor's order, the needles penetrate her with such force that they paralyse the place where she would react against the crime of her husband's friend. The nurse watches her moan. She hardly feels in her dying eyes the hatred that she has in her heart, to see herself forced to tolerate the presence of an enemy; especially in this corridor where she slips into her own debris, in this cold room where a machine sucks in her breath and pumps her blood.

The Haitian doctor begins to feel defeated. Marie-Anne resists his interrogation. His way to practise his science is by insulting his victim. Usually, the black woman admitted in his hospital answer his questions very nicely. Like a prisoner unsure of her defense. Like the child in order to soothe his conscience after two or three sins in the recreation yard. But today, things have changed. He is going to meet his first defeat, unable to extract a single word from the patient, unable to force her to pour her heart out; to remain standing in front of his victim without being able to make her turn around her dislocated image, or to lead her to see things according to the logic of another, to take on a colour other than her own, a reason other than her own, an identity that they want to give to women of her kind, for the women like Marie-Anne are about to upset the apple cart. Just a little bit more and the Haitian doctor would have struck the young woman. To make her unclench her teeth. If it weren't for the presence of the nurses he would have used the same methods used by the slave owners to untie the block's tongues, the accomplices of the runaways. He would have driven nails into the negress' head until she would spit out the truth, until she would admit to having helped a young man study medicine.

Doctor Hippolyte paces the room. He wants to try one last time to force the prisoner to confess her sins.

"Come now, let's be good. We want to help you. We can kill the bad spirit which is preventing you from speaking. Tell me your name. Have you a name?"

Marie-Anne is afraid of her resistance being broken. She makes an effort not to unclench her teeth, not to lose this power which keeps her hatred alive.

A breeze from the north blows between her numb legs; it brings her a little fresh air that she needs at the very moment where the density of her silence is measured to that of the revolution which is restrained in a scream jammed in her throat in order not to awaken the forces which are hostile to her liberation. She is about to make a sign to the nurse to give her a little water when the doctor's voice interrupts the communication.

"Nothing doing for the moment," he says to the intern. "She is possessed by a demon. She has the classic symptoms. Her eyes turn inside out; her looks go right through you like a savage's arrow. Her mouth is swollen. She is drooling. See how she is distorted in her ugliness and in her hatred for humans. When they are possessed, these negresses are the daughters of evil."

"According to you, Doctor, medical science has not yet succeeded in overcoming the mental illnesses in your country. Are the voodoo medicine men more competent than graduate doctors?"

"You cannot understand those things," retorted the doctor. "You see, the current hypothesis remains valid; the mental patients in Haiti are all followers of voodoo. How else can this woman's resistance be explained? Her demon paralyses her logical faculties: it gives her a limitless supernatural power."

"What power?" asks the Head Nurse.

"The one to defy science. Here are the precautions to take. Keep on the straight jacket; increase the morphine dose. I will recommend electric shock tomorrow."

The doctor gives one last glance at the patient. He goes out slamming the door.

Dr. Hippolyte's departure reduced Marie-Anne's tension. She regains her composure as well as the strength to control her nerves. The healer's words don't seem to affect her dignity as a woman. She thinks it's always the same image that is projected in a system whose three dimensions are negro factor, dirt and voodoo. It's always the same words put in the mouth of others, even in men of her race, for keeping the negress, the female, in her place.

In the hall the inmates cry out; they knit, they sing: *While going through Lorraine with my clogs* in order to go even farther than childhood. Her look slightly inclined toward one side of the sun, a young woman stays planted in front of Marie-Anne's room. Others, submitting to the routine of the words, imitate her gesture.

Until the sunset, the cleaning ladies are still sweeping to prevent the pollution of a theater set where beds become couches floating close to insanity. Nurses' aides will clean mirrors so that ex-ladies from Westmount will be able to find again their coquetry from before the Flood, to ease them in absorbing the electric shock, or to receive the messages sent by invisible voices.

Some women patients are talking to each other in the halls of the fifth floor. They are telling each other their adventures and they are playing with the last images they kept from the nightmares of the previous night. Heartbreaking stories are related: a disappointed husband has arranged for his wife to be put there before he went back to France to sign a contract with the president of a multinational company. For him, the fifth floor is more reassuring than his mansion in Westmount, where "madame" could, during his absence, flirt with just any pimp she would find. The ward inspires confidence to the jealous husbands; with its cohorts of security people, its priests, its forged iron fences, looking from top to bottom like unreachable towers.

The head nurse has a hard time to control the inmates. Some of the ladies are nervous. Some others are exhausted and empty after the electric shocks. At the nurses' station, a survivor from a concentration camp is reciting the code of laws of a fascist camp Kommandant. She is a frequent patient of the ward. When she can no more cope with her nightmare, she comes back to the ward to receive the morphine ration that will make it easier for her. She climbs on the front desk, waves her slipper to say goodbye to a security guard near the elevator. The smallest inducement makes her dance the polka. The doctors think that she has a strong anarchist tendency in her behaviour. She runs from one cell to the other in order to break the solitude. She is asked to go back to her own cell after her temperature is taken. It's high. The stern face of the doctor, this morning, makes her feel like breaking out. "I wanted to go," she says. "My body and soul are controlled by others. My breathing is also controlled by a machine."

Meanwhile, her neighbour is pulling her hair in desperation. She just had a terrible operation. Her husband had dreams of a less pointed nose. She went along with the idea. But the husband changed his mind. "The first nose was not so bad," he confessed. The poor girl went into a depression.

As the afternoon advances, the fifth floor becomes more and more like a beehive. That is because the evening is frightening, with its lines of ghosts, its busy downtown night clubs, its floating restaurants from the Queen Elizabeth where the gentlemen are drinking with their mistresses, and count the days until they could get rid of the corpse or the coffin of their mental patients. These ladies have a heavy heart, a breathtaking emotion, as we would have while listening to the crimes of a rascal.

As the tension among the inmates grows, and as the images of the patients are projected against the wall by the large light bulbs handled by the guards, Marie-Anne tries to find her way in this forest where only her shadow can be seen. She rolls and rolls her tongue in order to get rid of the taste of the medication prescribed by the Haitian doctor. She is conscious of the effects of this drug that has to be absorbed before the electric shock recommended for tomorrow morning. In a few hours she will be a vegetable. This damned treatment will take away her defence mechanism. He is going to make her roll over the mosaic of the ward, to make her lie about her delirium, about losing her will, or the broken pieces of the rules set by the golden jail where she is; he is going to make her dance on a hot beach at the tune of the rolling waves. "It's nice in prison," they will tell her. The true life is while you sleep. In the dislocation within yourself, in a dream without nightmares. They are going to make her sing "La Marseillaise" in créole, and see lovers kiss each other while the devil is laughing. They will tell her: "Get in Marie-Anne. Open your legs and let the doctor's snake come into you." They will tell her not to live with that hatred or this madness that others have created: an everyday madness, capable of bringing up smells that are incompatible with her dignity. They will tell her to be beautiful within an everlasting cowardice, to invent a language that is different from the torpor of her spirit, the vomit of her identity as a negress; she will have to learn to go deep within her sickness and discover the true image of her man.

Marie-Anne is fighting against the fear of losing her skin in the hands of the Haitian doctor. The two or three periods of lucidity she had during her fainting spell have shown her not to give in to the torpor of the medication. Nor to the beatitude of the machines. She will have to stay on the edge of the brook. She will have to compose her emotions, play within her madness in order to deceive the guards of the prison, to jump over the walls to find her freedom again, the freedom of a tracking dog looking for an escaped criminal.

The Haitian doctor comes back to the room of the patient. He feigns to act like her, to enter her skin, to imitate her speech, to identify with her sickness as if to show her his good faith before her misery, in this hall where time has stopped. Under the passive glance of the head-nurse, he stutters and starts a speech full of morals:

"Life is not all that bad." The doctor continued: "The sun always rises for the benefit of those who are ill because they are penitent and blessed with God's grace. Life is not that hard. Things are simple from the moment one knows what direction to take. The most important thing is to choose one's path, even though it is strewn with thorns, because basically, humanity needs people who are able to suffer for the good of others."

The head nurse covers her head. The words of the physician make her cry. Encouraged by the nurse's behaviour, he resumes his sermon.

"God alone knows the sacrifices that a black must have made to practice medicine today in a hospital this large. One need not envy the black physicians of this hospital because anyone can become one as long as he is willing to tear himself in two; in other words that he accepts sacrifices and suffering and then decided to go beyond these without letting his brain grow away from him with thoughts of unfaithful husbands, of white rivals, of life's problems, reflections of one's egoism; one must erase one's complexes, make the effort to forget the improprieties of others."

Marie-Anne does not turn her head this time. She looks at the physicians straight in the eye. She throws to his face the demonic fury of negresses when they revolt or break their chains. There is no doubt in the young woman's mind. Gros Zo said the same things in order to make her swallow his garbage. He had said "the world is sheer vanity, all is illusion and lies. Reality fools us every time. To have a drove of females at the fort would change nothing in the flow of time." Marie-Anne hadn't been mistaken. The Haitian physician is a traitor, a hypocrite, a liar, an oppressor of the race, like Gros Zo. Like Gros Zo as well, he wants to cajole his people, conceal from others his group's dirty needs. This physician, she thinks, is an accomplice of Gros Zo. The two are conspiring to make zombies out of women.

The physician remains silent. The patient keeps her dignity. She does not believe the solemn oaths, nor the knave who vomits on his colour the false complexes of the worthy man. He will leave the room as he came in as a well-dressed groom, thinks Marie-Anne.

Silence returns to the cell, a silence which contrasts with the seething within the young woman. Surely the physician will return after having recharged his batteries to impose a moral dimension on her decreptitude. She knows it; her resistance will have limits before the power of the healer. The only way, she thinks, to escape the tentacles of the physicians is to rid herself of her straight-jacket and chains. In the meantime she must play the role to the hilt. Like the doctor furthermore whose last words put to mind a scene from a play where the king mourns the death of a valet after he himself has cut his throat. One must feign death, thinks Marie-Anne, the adultress who has left one autumn night with a taxi driver. The doctor will have no difficulty making his diagnosis: acute neurotic crisis caused by absence of guilt. Race will have nothing to do with her insanity. Nor her colour. Nor her rage at seeing herself being treated like scum after having worked in factories for ten years in the United States to pay for Gros Zo's studies at Harvard university, after having forced her father to sell three hectares of land on the cul-de-sac plain to pay for Gros Zo's trips. These considerations are not taken into account in the treatment of neurosis. No more than the lessons in morality separating men into good and evil.

Marie-Anne thinks that she does not have the right to tell the doctor the truth about her pride as a black woman, the discredit she felt when she realized she was a slave, only good enough to allow herself to be closed into a house for a period of three hundred and sixty-five days. Because of her kinky hair, her plumpish body, and most of all her simplicity and her refusal to gossip in the company of high society women.

No. Things like this cannot be uttered. One can speak of hunger and thirst. However, one's shame at always having been ridiculed, abused, drawn into traps — these things one has to hide. Marie-Anne slowly begins to regain her strength. She will surely speak. But in a place other than the wing, down the same corridor where she experienced the depths of that pain which made her lose conmtrol, when she was found unconscious one beautiful autumn morning on a bench in a public park.

The noise of the inmates is no longer heard. Calm, it seems, has returned to the fifth floor; they must have found a way to tame the animals that were inciting the patients to overturn their beds and refuse their injections.

The head nurse enters Marie-Anne's room. Gently and with much tenderness, she makes her drink some water. She wipes her face with her hands, sits on the edge of the bed. The two women look at each other. Marie-Anne shudders. She tries once or twice to open her mouth. But the words remain stuck in her throat. And even if she could, she must hold herself back because the wing is under the control of the doctor. He and the nurse are of the same family, she thinks.

The nurse's face becomes more conciliatory. After making Marie-Anne's bed under the vigilant eye of a hefty warden, she places a hand on her chest.

"Are you hurting anywhere? What's wrong? You have to speak, you know! You were brought in this morning; you had lost consciousness. How can we help you?"

The young woman does not answer. She is contemplating the reflection of the sun pouring through the window of the room which, at this time in the afternoon, throws shadows along the walls and breaks the monotony of the objects like fireworks scattering fragments of light on the faces of children. She is lost in this decor where white and pink blobs are placed as in a painting, like pools swelling with the anger of the wind, or asymetrical points of dead branches falling into a cliff.

What hurts Marie-Anne the most is, no doubt, the block she creates for herself. When confronted with the facial expression of the head nurse, she finds it distasteful to have put the Haitian doctor and the head nurse in the same category, as if women, despite the colour of their skin, do not share the same language of pain, as if women have to foster the same collective suicides instigated by men for the salvation of the world.

The head nurse takes Marie-Anne's temperature a second time. She is not feverish. Yet she trembles at the idea of yielding before the nurse's tenderness. Putting her hand on the young woman's forehead, she makes her feel that she does not wish to harm her, that it is difficult at the beginning to get anything out of a new inmate because she is convinced the people in the wing are monstrous.

Despite these reassuring words, the young woman remains stone silent. She feels happier in her willful cultivation of her affliction, in a misery akin to that of a defeated male who, having beaten his female, goes and prays to Jesus Christ asking for even more strength so that he may kill her next time. Not being able to coax Marie-Anne, the head nurse leaves the room, not without reminding her that she must force herself to break the silence that encompasses her.

It is already six o'clock in the evening. Fear of the Haitian doctor plagues the young woman. Yet at the same time this fear gives birth to a hope that she can destroy the obstacles before her. She then starts to imagine an escape plan. She will admit her guilt at having assassinated her unfaithful husband. Her illness, she will tell the judge, is just a camouflage for her sin. She will be willing publicly to confess this sin as to the protestants of Haiti, as do the adulteresses in countries where people make love in the toilets of the feudal lord. She will also confess to her negro her debauchery in the offices of the minister who signed *monsieur's* passport!

Thus, early in the morning, the Haitian doctor will give a press conference on the situation of neurotic negresses who are incapable of adapting to a world of emancipated women. All will be in conformity with the municipal by-laws which forbid black women to raise their dresses to their chins in order to express their indignation at the betrayal by men of their race. There will then be a formal judgement from the Palace of Justice. Marie-Anne will be found guilty of having been a passive subject of a morbid imagination since her testimony could not resist the reality of the facts. For how would she convince a tribunal made up of doctors, men of worth, social workers with degrees, that a Black man, goodlooking, intelligent, a renowned physician, had locked up his wife in a room in the hope that she would commit suicide? Oh no! Such things are only invented for sensational films, for the kind of popular cinema where the mama accuses her negro of frinking all day long instead of working like a proper human being. *A doctor? Torturing his wife? Come on!* Will yell the first colleague called to the witness box. These are the intrigues of women who refuse to acquire polish and thus attain the stature of the liberated white women.

Moreover, Josette Ladouceur, a flighty brunette, learning of Marie-Anne's derailment this morning, has put in her two cents' worth. "Marie-Anne," she would say, "has remained under-developed; she might have taken a lover, given the impression that she accepted the exploits of her husband and have had a good time in her castle in Outremont, while he was doing the same at the cottage in Saint Agathe." For Josette Ladouceur, females always exaggerated more than necessary in order to gain the pity of others.

Marie-Anne's troubles won't be over, for the philosophers will rationally settle the issue: objective morality, they will say, ignores matters of sex. In a liberal society, one is free to have women no matter what their colour, their manner of seducing with their savage perfume, their smile, the trickery of elongating the face or of pretending to be innocent to snare men into their trap.

For the domestic triangle, or the decagon, the philosophers will thus continue by saying that the licentiousness of men and women has never stopped the world from turning round. It is necessary to liberate desire, to take the explosion of libido even further. Nothing must be held back, not even the beast in oneself that wants to take a woman while a first grade class watches.

And then there will be studies and investigations. In a year's time an advisory board, aware of the escalating number of mentally-ill negresses, will request Continuing Education of the University of Montreal to start a program to re-educate black women; they will be taught how to neutralize their impulses and water down their wine. "And, all the same, one must not exaggerate," said a political science professor. "A physician has both feet on the ground. Even if he did barricade one female in a room to go spend a few moments with another female, it is just the natural scheme of things. This proves that he is integrated; he does not drag his tribe behind him."

Thus, the dye was cast. Marie-Anne already knows what her sentence will be. One has to pay dearly for a scandal instigated in high scoiety. She must now pack and return home, where household events take place in the streets, where the father, mother, cousins, aunties and even the neighbourhood settle your account when you stay out all night or parade arm in arm with a mistress.

To the right and to the left Marie-Anne is cornered. Her decision is made. She will kill her negro. On another level, she has already killed him, as one kills a bad thoughts by replacing it with another evil thought, as one kills a father by imagining oneself to be the child of another. She will own up to her crime in front of the Haitian physician, the head nurse, the friends of her man who are omnipresent in the pavilion.

A noisy, grating adolescent, held by two men, is brought to the ward. The head nurse gives her some tranquilizers which she swallows without water, eyes closed with a sigh of satisfaction. Silently, she rolls herself into a ball on the hide-a-bed and whistles a popular tune. A few moments later, she sits up, stretches herself, sits on the edge of the bed. She takes her comb and smoothes her hair carefully. All of a sudden she sees Marie-Anne's silhouette in the mirror; she is being kept with the others despite her straight-jacket because, in the words of Doctor Hippolyte, it would be good for her to see how civilized beings live. Even in her madness she could learn something. The young girl gazes steadily at her and then says to her: "Tonight, I am going back home. If you like, I'll take you outside. You have to manage as best you can."

Without a further word, the two women sign a pact with their eyes. After the wardens' east round, Marie-Anne feels hands that are silent and free.

Quietly, she pulls from her nose and then from her head the tubes attaching her to a machine. Without a sound, she heads for the exit and, like an animal, the young woman makes a leap towards the nursing office. The nurse and three wardens remain completely motionless, astounded by such agility. Despite the pain in her stomach, Marie-Anne runs down the stairs at such a speed that she could have been taken for one of those possessed negresses who is capable of reaching the top of a high oak tree in a split second.

There she is, roaming through the corridors of the hospital basement. As if she were in a forest pulling outr bramble blocking her way, she wards off the iron bars at her head. Feeling that she is being pursued, the young woman hides in an office adjacent to the emergency room entrance.

The alarm is sounded. Policemen arrive to help the guards find the prisoner. The exits are blocked. Orders are given to be doubly watchful on the fifth floor of LaFontaine pavilion. Alone in an office, Marie-Anne takes a long while regaining her breath. From her throat come grunting sounds of pain, raw sounds like those of a mutilated prisoner. She examines her body, touching her legs where the imprint of the straight-jacket makes her cry for the first time. The young woman is bleeding, tired and trembling. A few minutes later, she is outside, quietly skimming the walls of the hospital.

POETRY

CLAIRE K. HARRIS

OBATALA

Obatala "who turns blood into children"
make me a man out of my blood
Out of his bones make me a son
A son with his head and his hands and his feet
A son who can place brick upon brick
and yet read from a book.
A man of his grandfathers and of their wisdoms
And still a man with the light of dawn on him
Grant him old age and grace.
Obatala "who rests in the sky like a swarm of bees"
If you will not grant me all these
grant me at least a child
so that my blood will not curdle with shame
Or I grow deaf waiting to hear love call my name.

BLOOD FEUD

after the savage rites the moon red in her ears   small reward
for bruised lips against the pane the moon huge, blood red
and singing   above, a cloud black as a fist

lifted she knows flesh is not civilized flesh is not haiku
despite the red surge in the mouth   brutal hope despite her
fury   the skin alert to the body's clear voice   across the sky
quicker than in her own dance the moon rose   passed above the
pines   so his eye held above her   his dark attentions

paid, the judas flesh wet churned into rush and breaking   it
was always thus   the brain's clear anger, the body's welcome   and at such times   the moon full blurred and singing

OUTPORTS

In charity   from these skull crags   wind drowned raw boulder
fields   these coves   and small earth-filled patches   they
plucked the islanders

These fishers   dwellers of the green grey ocean world   who clung
gnarled   who rocked by waves   preyed on fish and lobster   lashed
by sleet   frozen white bearded death   pain prodded   bark stubborn   grand   grand survivors grown hard and grey ocean calm
carried by storm and ice   they moved in star motion as all birthed
to cliff and deep water   who know drowned hair snarls on shoals
eyes turn to moon   where maybe men have walked and maybe not
Their cliff havens wooden white lace at window panes and faces
the bone cold's slow dissolving before the wood stove   the axe
the fiddle   the silent confidences spilled over deaf tables

in charity   they were uprooted the Islanders to the bright terylene
world   delivered to TV and the still land   the mail too is delivered
   the flesh pales and slips

DANIEL CAUDEIRON

MY LOVE IS AN AFRICAN WOMAN

Sensuous, serene, and secure;
her aura is music, the pulse of the drum,
windborne whisper of wild spirits,
secret ceremonies, the shaman's song.

My Love, an African princess,
a phoenix surmounting the townships and shebeens,
shaming the sham of surrounding decay;
her vibrance, her queendom,
mock the terror of batons and pistols;
survivor her splendour, eternal and free.

My Love, an African temptress,
her hips are fluid and fulgent,
fountain, shoshona, fulcrum of quilla,
the rhythm of dance.
Her lips are nectar pits, renewing, redeeming,
the locus, the focus of love.

My Love, an African songbird,
her voice is wild desert honey,
laced with liquid fire,
scalding and stubborn, and soothing.
Azanian melody, ancient and wise,
her core is clicking laughter,
her warmth is shelter,
enveloping and perpetual.

My Love, an African Sphinx,
mystery and distance and magic,
turns my blood to strong wine,
to ambitious river-rush, overspill.
Her presence is blessing, is balm, is black;
My love is an African queen
Yah bo. Yah bo.

COMPULSION

Really, you are the blue dome,
the wind, the seed.
You slip through my fingers.
All of you, over my heart
gilds the mountains,
gives the brightness to my eyes;
knot up the strands of my hair.
Nude, you run thick, hot in my blood;
you are green in the trees,
and over me, over my world, you are huge.

I see in you the birds,
hear the joyous air of mariners
when they break port,
and with the irregularity of a star
I consume myself
over the topography of your flesh.

Then, O then, I am naked, aglow within
your embrace,
warm and scented clean,

And I sail in your waters free;
or shipwrecked, adrift, I cling for life
to your word,
to your two agile legs
so that you may know
that I am yours
through both the night and the air.

Come, come let us go through the woods and parks,
where sunlight streams,
and the lawn takes shelter in your arms,
where you may extend yourself in offering
unmindful of all else,
because I am the master of your aura,
through which my blood circulates . . .

with my profound insomnia
my lucid silences
and my long, lone exile.

DAY SHIFT/NIGHT SHIFT

At Queen and Spadina,
the traffic thunders on, squeezing left
for road repairs, Babylon and Babel converge,
near misses, kissing fenders, *aqui se habla espanol.*
fala Portugues,
chinese varieties, jamaican groceries,
A permanent crush,
all day rush.

But at night,
the neon kids are out to play,
light up the pavement,
trendy music, trendy food,
wearing out the Shoe
with reggae high-spanks,
luminous makeup,   punk masks,
the earache,
the   mind grind of soHo,
the newest wave to crash . . .

English broken here.

MARLENE NOURBESE PHILIP

ODETTA

Bareback
it rode
the raw blue words
bucking and twisting
in the grip of pure sound
this voice ambushed
somewhere
between the Cape of Good Hope
and the Mediterranean
between the Atlantic
and the Indian Ocean
fired in the New World
bareback it rode
the raw blue words
the blackstrap burnt sugar
field holler catching the power
all right I'm coming Lord voice
of reggae, calypso mento and ska
the canefield cottonfield
chitlins souse blackpudding
peas an' rice voice
of the freight train
I'm never coming back
I've got the Monday morning blues voice
of the lynch mob
the what'll I have for this big buck
and here's a good breeder voice
the voice of
I'm going to North America to make my fortune
we shall overcome
when will it all end
of the black and beautiful
right on gimmie five
rhythm and blues
that wants a piece of the action

E. PULCHERRIMA

I came awake —
swimming in a pool of blood
was the poinsetta
e. pulcherrima
Euphorbia Pulcherrima —
most beautiful Euphorbia
the poinsetta

comes in to her passion
comes in to her own
passes her blood
normally
naturally in the tropic
days and nights of equal length
pools of blood
seeping slowly through
barking backyards
swiftly spreading
her menstrual stain
reddening finicky frontyards
hedges trying to hide
her touch
seducing children
their fingers sticky with her milk
old men
dagger eyes glazed with age
and lust weaned too soon
from her adhesive breasts
until she will be denied no more
before the cock crow breaks
the day into two impossible halves
she sashays into town
has to be forgiven seventy times seven

for that blood
that red
that poinsetta

e. pulcherrima
she bleeds
unseen

uncared for
unloved
untouched
understood and vice versa
"and if you cut her back
before her time of month
she bleeds even more —
just like a woman"

the blood
the red
poinsetta
e. pulcherrima
loosening her red
her blood
laughter over the sun stunned land
the suddenrains shocked into silence
her white sticky milk
gumming up the works
feeding and bleeding
bleeding and feeding

her blood
her red
poinsetta

e. pulcherrima
Euphorbia Pulcherrima
alias Mexican Flameleaf
alias Lobster Flower
alias Christmas Flower
description: a tall bright bush
identifying marks: flames
wanted possibly for imitating
the voice
the passion
the birth and death
the body, the blood of life
her dossier reads
"imitatio christi"
the north fears her

second coming prismed
in all of the above

"all that blood —
that red"

she heard the bloodcall
gives the response
— was the chance of a lifeline —
— to enter —
immediately she calls
into question
the bloodless snows
the shrieking silence
the hollow rings of emptiness
spotting with her blood
she refuses —
refuses to bleed
within
or without
her lover
will not be
unfaithful
will not die
will not bleed

the blood
the red
poinsetta

e. pulcherrima
insists on her rights
to privacy
to darkness
to silence
to blackness
(albeit makebelieve)
all of the above or none
insists on her right
not to bleed
not to feed
for fourteen out of every
twenty four hours
not to feed or bleed

the blood
the red
poinsetta

e. pulcherrima came awake
in a pool of blood
birth blood
trickling down
thickening thighs
sticky
with her hot milky sap
spilling from broken limbs
milked white
forgot the sticky fingered children
(they were really only stick children)
where were the old men?
forgot her lover
(he came to her for twelve hours at a time)
was forced to bleed
the buds of blood
the blood of red
the blooded poinsetta
an immaculately forced conception
there was no annunication
only a joyless mating
of light and darkness
in the ice wounded womb
she finally bled
e. pulcherrima

Euphorbia Pulcherrima
also known as
Mexican Flameleaf
Lobster flower
Easter Flower
Christmas Flower
never as the Bleeding Flower

a tall bright bush
a flame
a woman
e. pulcherrima
she finally bled.

SALMON COURAGE

Here at Woodlands, Moriah,
these thirty-five years later,
still I could smell her fear.
Then, the huddled hills would not have
calmed her, now as they do me.
Then, the view did not snatch
the panting breath, now, as it does
these thirty-five years later, to the day,
I relive the journey of my salmon mother.

This salmon woman of Woodlands, Moriah
took the sharp hook of death
in her mouth, broke free and beat
her way upstream, uphill; spurned
all but the challenge of gravity,
answered the silver call of the moon,
danced to the drag and pull of the
tides, fate a silver thorn in her side,
brought her back here to spawn with
the hunchbacked hills humping the horizon,
under a careless blue sky.

My salmon father now talks of how
he would walk over there, to those same hills,
and think and walk some more with his dreams,
then that he had,
now lost and replaced.
His father (was he salmon?)
weighted him with the millstones of
a teacher's certificate, a plot of land
(believed them milestones to where he hadn't been),
that dragged him downstream to the ocean.

Now, he and his salmon daughter
face those same huddled, hunchedbacked hills.
She a millstoned lawyer, his milestone
to where he hadn't been.
He pulls her out, a blood rusted weapon
to wield against his friends —
"This, my daughter, the lawyer!"
She takes her pound of dreams neat,
no blood under that careless blue sky,

100

suggests he wear a sign around his neck,
'My daughter IS a Lawyer,'
and drives the point home,
quod erat demonstrandum.

But I will be salmon.
Wasn't it for this he made the journey
downstream, my salmon father?
Why then do I insist on swimming
against the tide, upstream,
leaping, jumping, flying, floating,
hurling myself at, under, over,
around all obstacles, backwards
in time for spawning
grounds of knotted dreams?
My scales shed, I am Admiral red,
but he, my salmon father, will not
accept that I too am salmon,
whose fate it is to swim against the tide,
whose loadstar is to be salmon.

This is called salmon courage my dear father,
salmon courage,
and when I am all spawned out
like the salmon, I too must die —
but this child will be born,
must be born salmon.

CYRIL DABYDEEN

RUM-RUNNING

A Martimer's new life —
I am at the edge of my seat; water boiling
Mud slaking.

A kiln's turn-around
At the city's end. Fumes rise up
And swirl

Across the ocean, Atlantic's swell
And billow. I taste cod
In Jamaica, Barbados, Trinidad
And Demerara — more trade. In Newfoundland
Later, I lie drunkenly —

Wind wafting. Whole fields of sugar-cane
And beet. Backyard and tenement
Hear the police siren. Now run, man!

An urchin's scampering feet,
Shirt tails flying in the wind.
Such ragged talk afterwards, scattering
Fowls, ducks. A goat's lone grunt

Good as a bray. I hold on to a wad of notes
Like a tufted beard, dancing my way
To paradise. Half-sotted, I echo disdain —
I continue to make-believe

Patterning myself whole, dreams coming
Alive across the ocean, a ship canting;
Land lifting up, the fumes yet in my nostrils,
My body's own heat —
I continue to rise like yeast.

SIR JAMES DOUGLAS: FATHER OF BRITISH COLUMBIA

("What a good a little molasses
can do.")

1

You were born where I was born.
Demerara's sun in your blood,
Guiana's rain on your skin.
You came from Creole stock
taking a native wife
who hardly shadowed your
British pride
    with the 'dougla' taint.

You are part of my heritage too
despite colonialism
and bending to the rule
for a while.

2

Fever on the Frazer river now:
Victoria's ribbed veins
pulsated with the gold lust.

Settle dispute after dispute
with the Haidas;
sweet smell of molasses
in their veins, rum
dizzying their minds
while each jewel
formed the dung heap
of another claim.

They come from everywhere.
Ah, keep the Americans out;
let the rabble stay far and wide
(de Cosmos loudest of all).

3

El Dorado of a different kind now.
Note the natives coming out

of their dark days after
the era of the Hudson Bay Co.
and colonial
        administration

And I remember pouring sugar
in my tea in St. Mungo's city
where you were educated,
thinking if you were more Scottish
I'd be less of the tropics.

LENIN PARK, HAVANA

My camera flashes upon the variegated faces
Amidst the general activity
Of building, establishing —
How eager they are, these hands, bodies —
Nine —, ten — and eleven-year-olds
Bustling about without weariness —
Only a restrained air of the carnival
Of the young
                    this summer.

I will speak. "Hola," in bare Spanish
Eager to find out how the socialist man
Or woman can transform a state;
In command's way, they seem not to mind —
Innocence has its own currency, as I watch
A young girl driving a tractor,
A boy milling rice; another, refining sugar.

Will they ever starve, as they pay tribute
To José Marti, Fidel Castro, or whoever else
Will be then? Or will some stalwart spirit
Among them, given to brooding —
Later high on culture, insist on the right
To be free beyond bread?

Doubtful as I am, I banter, smile;
My camera snaps again, left and right —
Those black hair bordering beautiful
Dark and brown faces — I love you all;
A hybrid breed chockful of Latin air —
Among you, perhaps, are eager dancers,
Singers, poets — how elegantly you proclaim
An island in the pulsation of your bodies,
In the greater exaltation of spirit yet to come
Far beyond Castro or Marti.

(July 14, 1982)

MY COUNTRY, NORTH AMERICA, AND THE WORLD

With a dune of sugar the imagination
Licks itself: the heart beats faster —
The Middle Passage's below deck

With Raleigh at the Orinoco, take me as I come,
Indentured or indigenous,
Whose world?

Again crossings: the new rises up;
I am a Parliament breed, lurching forward
With Canning, Buxton, Wilberforce —

The dark's passing passion.
Now in the Great White North, striving
For the albino state, I will soon be perfect

Without piquancy; what's ahead of us?
It is you I fear most, you who I
Think of constantly —

Falling prey to deeper sins, far beyond
The Commandments, blindfolded,
Covered with blood

Let me walk a straight path
Let me come to you with only
A sharp tongue

I will reach those limits where
I will only protest with the cry
Of peace, finally

ABDUR-RAHMAN SLADE HOPKINSON

THE COMPASS

You blew a pair of bubble gametes; crammed them
With diagrams like winged coils; married them,
And lo! I was. Egg, leech, fingerling, as if in summary
Repeating time's long stages. You hardened
My skeleton. You ribbed and jointed it;
Encased my brain in bone. You fleshed me out; you nerved me
For my grand entrance. You tuned my voice
To squall, to gurgle, chuckle, laugh outright;
Steadied my wobbling eyes with focussed sight;
Exalted me upon the prongs of choice.

O perfect sweetness! Adult, errant will,
My fuel and compass. Never mind the Hob-Godling
That lurches out of childhood. Rolling-calf,
Bush Beast-ghost, blood-red-eyed, with a din of chains,
Old Duppy-King, lord of a dripping jungle
Where fears huddle or scurry.
                              "Me nah 'fraid You!
Me walk where me foot tek me, or me mind."

I slicked my hair, deciduous now, and grey.
You never turned. It was I who turned away.

One day, abruptly I reversed my feet;
Sought Your direction — so said my conceit.
Anticipator! O, You nudged me, planted
That seed and yearning; yet, from Your Graciousness,
You credit me the sowing.
Did the double prong of choice fuse to one tine
At my decision? No.
There's no contending with Your stern arrest.
To You, like a plain needle, I incline
From Your magnetic virtue, not from mine.

1968

I home towards islands, where the sea
Will rinse my restless, bathing eye,
With continental mud now too long blind;
And where, not sour, root-strangling clay,
But loam, friable with humus, chipped shell, sand,
Will bed my crops under the green day;
And O, again, blue sea,
Medicinal essence of earth's rind,
Will cauterize my cloven mind.

SNOWSCAPE WITH SIGNATURE

Against the snow-hill
A rime-clad tree, like branched and crusted crystal.
On mid-branch,
A bird, a brush-stroke
Fluffs at the cold.
At the hill's foot struggles
An ice-arrested stream.
"Whooooo?" asks the wind, rhetorically.
"Wherever you turn; there is a signature
On star, and starry snowflake. Whose?" The question
(A frosty, shuddering aria on the wind)
Praises His contrapuntal, terse design.

LILLIAN ALLEN

MARRIAGE

When mi sidown
Pon mi bombo claat
in a calico dress
under the gwango tree
a suck coarse salt
fi the night fi dun
wen twist face joan
and mi man mus come
down those concrete steps
from her tatch-roof house
han in han an' smile
pon them face

An a bus'im 'ead
wid a cistern brick
blood full mi yeye
a tear 'er shut
rip 'im pride
the little heng pon nail

The two rocky miles 'ome
we drop some fists
Blood soaked licks
Kasha sticks

But later on
a sooth 'im pain
bathe the blood down
the cistern drain
ten common-law-years
ina wi tenament yard

An sure as 'ell
wi anger rest
'im eyes regret
plea 'an confess
then glide mi

to gramma dead-lef bed
an' marry mi
under the chinelle spread
again an' again
'till day does done
evening come

BELLY WOMAN'S LAMENT

A likkle seed
Of her love fi a man
Germinates in her gut
She dah breed
Cool breeze
It did nice
im Nuh waan no wife
Just life
Wey Fi do!

The likkle seed
jus a grow
bloat her belly
It noh know
How it change
Mek life rearrange

Ooman bruk
Nuh likke wuk
Man gawn
Nuh waan noh ties
just life
Wey Fi doh!

Anada heart
Start fi beat
Anada mouth
de fi feed
Plant corn
Reap weed

Wey fi doh!

HORACE GODDARD

MAMAETU

My mother worked
mother land
in hand-
fuls of
chop chop

She sailed her hoe
Damballa Damballa
above and below
Damballa Damballa
in scorched fields
sowing seeds
for zombies

On the fallow
Ogun Balanjo
on the ground
Ogun Balanjo
pound after pound
of hand digging
of widening
trenches
she plucked the weeds
planted the seeds
and waited

Oh iponri
Oh iponri
Damballa Hwedo
Ogun Batala
Ogun Balanjo
Damballa Hwedo

Mother, we are here

CONCH-SHELL

Carapace of crab
lamefoot scab
and the infant's face
bulges with a taste
of corn pone
of cassava pone
of prime-ribbed aloes
and the hurt
of shoe-cracked toes

Jungle trees jingle
corner shops single
out the niggers
fuh rum in jiggers
an' massa he sips
gin an' lemon
while he han's get busy
searchin' the folds of Susy
nature, breeding frowsy —
smellin', doan bade,
red-haired litters

de Royal Bank summon dem
Barclays wine and dine dem
Fogarty's welcome dem
fuh snatch de purses
fuh catch de curses
of black nannies
counting dem pennies

CHARLES ROACH

POEM TO BUDDY EVANS

dear buddy
the shot that bust your heart
singed the city
we are fighting we are hot
and we will not be stopped buddy buddy

six badges and six guns
were there to fell you
and leave you in
the disco dust to die

and in the streets
we said we won't forget you
for on every poor man'd head
a rubber stamp repeats buddy buddy

black buddys white buddys
yellow and red and brown buddys
wherever rich and poor
are separated by the law

the stinking inquest
stings our nostrils
an obscene spectacle
where cops choose the prosecutor judge and jury

shoot justify cover-up lie
shoot justify cover-up lie
lie lie lie lie

coroner crown and cop
feast like vultures
first they stripped your bones
then started on your lawyers

emerging arm in arm
crown and coroner
from behind closed doors
announcing vindication

people lodge complaints
and no one listens
will their rage dry up
or bust out like a bomb?

will your name buddy
be repression's bullseye
or will it be
a people's battlecry?

DANIEL CAUDEIRON

CARIBANA: TORONTO

Love
plus
soul
plus
black, white
plus
colours that
fascinate, captivate.
Colours that splash
plus calypsoes
that suffer from
the energy crisis
plus
band fiascos
plus
butterflies, plus
rain, plenty rain,
down the main
plus costumes,
cylinders and wings
flags, sequins, banners
plus
oranges
grapefruits
lemons, pumpkins and coconuts
plus
scantily clad beauties,
the crisis being beaten

Macho rum and big bass drum
pounding across the mind,
the borders afar
plus water
plus rain
pouring down the main drag
on University on the city
torrents and buckets
plus amnesia
due to extravagant
intoxication

a waft of weed smoke
and you know why
everybody look like joke.
Colours
a magnificent splash
a rainbow varsity
rhapsody at Queen's Park
first time ever

Kisses
sessions
that last for hours
in spite
of the weather
the paraders were
on the move
up and together
under escort,
Toronto moving
southbound
colours
bodies
spare parts
prancing entrancing grandstanding
rolling to the beat
synchronized
bodies exposed
sensationally
and I jumping
jovial
frantic
excited
kingdom come
calypso sweet.

A dream filled with life
plus
truth
plus
soul.

The sun at last
bearing down
heat on the street
raising banners
blood rising

drums hypnotizing
strong as ever
devilry on Dundas
whistles shrilling
music killing.
Soca, it's yours
you're beautiful
Caribana,
those who jump in it
love it
because
Soca soul
plus more soul
plus
flashy floats
plus rhythm
plus
steel that rings deep.

DIONNE BRAND

P.P.S. GRENADA

I have never missed a place either
except now
there was a house
there was a harbour, some lights
on the water, a hammock
there was a road,
close to the cliffs'
frequent view of the sea
there was a woman
very young
her boy much older,
we planted corn and ochroes
and peas in the front garden
though the rats ate the corn
there was a boat,
I made friends
with its owner and he called
me on his way to work each morning
there was another road, the one to Goave,
all the way up looking back
the rainy season greened the hills
dry spells reddened the flamboyant
there was a river
at concord
seeing it for the first time surprised me
big smooth stones, brown and ashen
and women standing in its water
with washing
there was a farm
on a hillside
as most are, forty acres with a
river deep inside, Jason and Brother-
man picked coconuts, the air,
the brief smell of cloves, Rusty
swam naked in the river's pond
after our descent, Jason's room
reminded me of a house when I was
a child, wooden windows, dated magazines
books and no indoor tap,
there was a wall of rock which sank into the street

in the trees and vine and lizards
it cooled the walk from town,
though town was hot and steep whenever I
got to the market it was worth the task,
there was a spot, in the centre of the women
and the produce, near to the blood pudding vendor
a place where every smell of earth and sweat
assailed the nostrils and the skin, I would
end up coming home, with the scrawniest provisions,
I don't know how, it was those women's eyes
and their hands, I'd pass by the best and
buy from the most poor,
there was a tree
at the head of the beach,
Grand Anse, not in a showy spot
but cool and almost always empty
of tourists
the ocean there was calmer, shallow,
more to Filo's liking
sea grapes, that was what the tree grew
sea grapes, not at all like grapes in north america
a tougher skin, a bigger seed
sweet and sour at once,
there was the carenage, street and harbour
dock and motorway
tied up to it sometimes 'the sea shepherd'
'albatross' 'Vietnam' 'alistair'
the boats to Carriacou, banana boat, the 'geest' and
the tourist boat — Cunard, envy and
hatred to these last two
"how many rooms in that boat, you think?"
this from Frederick, he's had to sleep in
one with his mother and her husband
and when they come down from country,
two more children.
there was a street
a few more really, perhaps
twenty or so would be accurate, inclined, terraced,
cobbled or mud
when I first saw them I remember blanching
at the labour and resolve required to climb them
I would give more than imagined to see them
as they were,
there was a night swimming in the dark
grande anse, morne rouge, la sagesse, with voices
after and brandy,
there was a woman thin and black like

a stick, though she mistrusted me, a foreigner,
I marvelled at her
there was a friend,
named for a greek,
storyteller like his namesake Homer
he would promise a favour this afternoon
and return five days later with a wild tale
about his car, his hands, the priorities
of the revolution and his personal safety
or a fight with his uncle.
the post office, its smell of yellowing paper,
stamps, its red iron mail box, wooden
posts, the custom's house, its stacks
of paper filled out by hand in quadruplicate,
its patience, its frustrated waiting lines
lunch hour, noon to one, everything is shut
the day's heat at its triumph,
there was a path
wet with grass, weedy
stones but people rarely walk there preferring
the high path overlooking the town,
another thing,
on woolwich road, the view on its left
incline, houses leaning down, lines of clothing
pots and flowering brush, the ever present
harbour framed through bits or wide angled
to point salines,
there was an hour actually many when
the electricity broke down,
my sister grew angry and I lit candles
and the lamps
looking forward to their secretness,
even when the electricity returned
and all around put on their fluorescent lights
I left the candles burning.
there was a month when it rained
and I did not have an umbrella
or proper shoes,
more pot holes appeared in the streets
and pumpkin vines grew swiftly over Marlene's
doorstep,
that was when the sand in the ocean shifted
and levelled out the deep shelf,
that was when the sea became less
trustworthy,
after Dominica, St. Lucia, St. Vincent
I came back with such relief I

talked to the taxidriver from Grenville
all the way home,
Birch Grove, Beaulieu
after Vieux Fort and Marigot this was comfortable.

ARNOLD ITWARU

RAGBLOWN ROADLESS

ragblown roadless
these men wheeze under dying trees

their barnyard cackle rattles
the hollows of their evening
flesh eating bone

across the buckling bridge
dry rain in calabash skulls
branded speechless
tomorrow's women empire-cursed
strike their womb's dream
eyes lowered

old paint defaces the towns
the villages are decrepit shelters
where the old dream of yesterday
and yesterday and of their children
fled Toronto-London way

blow softly on them Atlantic
soften their sleep
and their tomorrows

THE FAITHFUL

Matin mornings in cowpasture days,
confession behind wax-smelling altars,
dead man spreadeagled on a cross.

The brethren sing sweet Jesus walking Galilee,
they hear the slurp-slap of mud in the footpaths
of sleep, their cries Legioned in sugarcane fields,
calypsoes, rum, Saturday night brawls.

Confess, rumbles the pulpited ghost, breathing sin,
redemption, eternal blemish. Deflowered on damp pews
the brethren of little faith confess sun-cursed sins,
they know "how sweet the Name" sounds in believers' ears.
They confess, unworthy servants,
servants scratching palms.

The morning drinks them up and moves on.

EDWARD A. WATSON

THE SONG MY LADY SINGS

And all they wish to tell now
are stories about the bad times
and what a little spoon light did for you
and how you choked on too much stuff
awakening to drawn-out pre-dawn silences
blinking past the sleep of too many drinks
or how you pulled yourself together
trying to reach after certainties
'til the curtain fell
as if your life was separated completely
from your singing
like last year's paid up bills
some marked "received in full"
others simply "paid"
dues they say
ironic tragic
vain victories
worn out by too much remembering

And they never talk about
your shaking your head
wanting to despise the perfect
positioning of the rings
on your fingers and around your eyes
trying to say hello and goodbye
to heartache
in one tremulous tear
or how you smiled
for the gardenias
dazed from too much rain
in the small garden
and for the sweet sad mouthing of love
nowhere like the perfect articulation
the perfect harmony
borne by violets flaunting furs
and snow even then
had so many meanings
like love
euphoric sad passive aching

And now

even after all the good times
they could never write
the right words for you
for it was always life that played
the song my lady sings.

BEYOND THE REACH
OF THE FARTHEST DREAM

In the untidy year of my birth,
they murdered Garcia Lorca in a forest
of stark pines, and the women of Guernica
wore their hatred like granite across
the petrified landscapes of Spain.

Forty years after Lorca
and three years after Neruda left us,
I began my torturous pilgrimage
in the tactless parsimony of
Out of the Silent Stone.

(An' w'en a read de t'ing in Jamaica,
dem say: He does not live here.
An' a read it in Canada, an' dem say:
He does not live here.
A read it in Washington, D.C., an' dem say:
He does not live here.)

Here is the privilege of not suffering
through the mighty frustration of
the dry wind; the not glorying in
the Anglo-Blackson identity carved
out of snow and autonomous provinces;
here is the capital capitol's arrogance
of the blind man's parochial truth.

No matter.   I can afford to be extravagant with life's extravagances,
for in the thirty-eighth year of his life
they murdered Frederico Garcia Lorca
in a forest of stark pines.

Each day, each month, each year bears
its tragedies, and each reverberation
reaches each of us here in the deepest
valley of our suffering. From every
gesture, every posture, we fashion the
history of our lives, and each man's vision
ranges far beyond the simple reach of words,
beyond profitless love
and the intimacies of loneliness:
desire, adoration, then stillness.

Without passion, the poem in each of us
dies a contemptible death.

Yet *they* belong. *They* are the sons
and daughters of place, marking their lives
by the ritual succession of things:
to be baptized
to be confirmed
to be thankful
to be wedded
blind, always blind, to the leavening
of beauty with the yeast of their anger
and their despair.

But we are the outsiders
and we shall seek the splendid city,
even where the far horizon swallows
the oceans and the seas;
and we need to die for causes,
gasping like the drowned sun
in an endless grave of salt and sand.

Instead,
let metaphor stand and serve openly.

Of brine and grit are the pillars of love
erected;
out of the dark ineffable wonders
of the heart are the songs of despair
created;
out of death's intangible vocabularies
are the dirges of loss
inflected;
out of the skill of Nature's alterations
are the odes of praise
generated:

these are the poems of life and of death.

And if we must go down,
let us not go down in old metaphors
("to the sea in ships"),
but beyond . . . beyond
the reach of the farthest dream
here the man struck dumb
though he remains dumb
mumbles his words forever
in the volcanic blood
of the world's jealous body.

KARL GORDON

STRANGERS AT A GLANCE

Against an ocean's mind
You would deny us
This vast expanse
Of arable dreams

This vast, unending acreage
Of fertile hope
You would deny us

Yet even now her plains
In winter's garb,
Smiling, beckon us
To share her snow
And quiet fields
Eloquent
With stark silhouettes
Of monumental pines
And future sighs

Even the wind whispers
A welcoming blast
To the chilling spectre
Of our unaccustomed presence

But tomorrow
It will be spring
And tomorrow
Life begins anew
In its hopeful struggle
To find the promised warmth,
This strange new clime.

Not so long ago
Birds and other fragile beings,
Unnatural though it seemed,
Had braved her forbidding winter's whip
And succumbed to her insistent cooing

And now, we too
Have fallen under her spell
Her mountains luring to the challenge,
The true north majestic, viselike
Magnetizing to a final reckoning

OLYMPIC DREAM

Strength I ask
To dismiss this rudeness
That would otherwise make me blush
With the muted fury of angry words

Strength I ask
To understand the ignorance
That disguises our common bond
By magnifying these pointless differences

Strength I ask
To control this hand raised high
in senseless passion to extinguish
The arrogant boldness of your cheek

Strength I ask
To silence the effrontery
That would banish tolerance
From this eternal well-spring of hope

With failing strength
To you we give this torch
Ensuring that the light will always shine
For those whose simple faith believes our dream

ANTHONY PHELPS

THE FATHER'S MOUTH

translated by Colette Pratt

Ithaca Ithaca
sings the shrewish hour
In the tender core of the underbark
the sap no longer lends an ear
to the jabbering tadpoles
The rapid notes of the thrush
encode a salted noon

For once the naked tree
crosses the forest
its head a pharaoh's
I struggle
and unfold like a bud
and for the sea
my back an inkstand

Oh
to ensnare one word
of this galloping phrase which breaks
and reshapes itself furiously
One word
one number
my living man's epitaph
But I can reveal little
that the roundness of the note doesn't tell
Annihilated Babylon
petrified Pompeii
the river Tage counting its dead
purple ridge or desert
the serpent goddess from the depth of her display case
can't go on anymore
knows not what to invent
the cornstalk's alphabet cannot spell out all the sap

And the huge avid leaf
low wall between continents
pursues its incessant tattoo
so that the stone and the froth may cross
under the decaying light

until the day when the sun
will contemplate our planet
seduced by its mad children
under the spell of the trumpets of Patmos

Father my double
at this rift before everything totters
my vision burgeons
with all the ash-headed men
silicon chompers
or worshippers of the feathered serpent
gauche descendants of demi-gods
custodians of ruins

At this low land stop
in all these chosen places of living stones
or petrified times
I shape identical images
shaking my memory
with a great din of leaves and rattling
for the satisfaction of the beggar in myself
lavish with his rags

Sand-headed intellectual with nailed feet
anxious hip
I walk like a persistent root
my head engulfing the obstacle
I scrape the living bones
my rough hand
jackhammer nail
i insist
I make headway
risking a tempting word
but already my saliva transforms it into limestone

O Babel of Herodius Atticus
the Parthenon gives birth to backward divinities
and the echo from the Escorial filters a senile voice
from the Alhambra to the Acropolis
the new agoraphobic masters rule

May the vigilant bull's horns
rip open once and for all the acrobat of knossos
and Dedalus-Labyrinth will only be a fable
for wool spinners or tireless goatherds
moving monoliths of a degraded scenery

But where then is the tragic
and where the opposition?

Oh peace in the name of the rosemary
to the navigator staggering on fettered horses
Peace in the name of the child with the hoop
to the awkward lamb on the straw
My hybrid brothers
keepers of arenas
watch over the night of cacti
and at the entrance of the icon
where the prophets keep guard
the girl of the naked bulb
lives her cinematic dream
false disco Garbo

Veiled Father
my other mutant face
for once the drop is exploring the ocean
drowned sceneries
annotated dragon teeth
I ascend as a flowery profile
worthless bearer of thrones and dominions
my bowl in white satin
in votive rustling like death
and my hand describes without stopping
its great bannerlike phrase

But the stutterers of exile
these long children with dead eardrums
don't decipher the flight of the calico-bird
For them changing past
entangled words
falling like seagulls with buttered wings
grail-country between two rounds of leap-frog
For once the image has rejoined its source
dangerous crossing of the other
as a mirror
as frozen water
the sheep unties its spool
in the tempo of flutes
of pulleys
idols
moth-eaten masks
crosses
pleated jabots
silicon tar
hawthorn and clog
up to where savannah roots
up to where

My Lent purged I readjust myself
without echo or support
my memory as in blindman's buff
And he who goes with knife-steps under my window
my song rubs him out
trapped hunter dead in the gunsight's center

Oh Father my witness face
I've freed myself
from the ditches and walls of childhood
and here I am the eye of reason in my pocket
pacing the domain of ripe age
from the woman's night song
to the diurnal dance of mica
from the scratching of the sign
to the militant gesture
and I plant my rose at all corner cafés
where my wife with brown socialist eyes
shares by my side
the wine and the brocade

O attic of ripe age
land finally recognized
great leafy word
I am no longer the blind man
moving between marshes
and quicksands
opening up space with weak arms and trembling fingers
but the one who forces fate
and traps and counters it
the Exiled of disturbed roots
masturbating and incestuous
I
the single and the double
the Hermaphrodite eating stuffed grape leaves
at the base of every acropolis

I am no longer of this nomadic race
surveyors of the horizon and diggers of sand
with my amulet hand I push aside the basilisk
I exorcise
and unfettered
all tethers cut
I ford the exile
like a crackling presence

O attic of ripe age
inventoried without complacence
I fearful decapode

134

stunned chrysostom of a new mermaid song
to the incense of lost steps
I regain a dream country
so desired
where each crochet motion
renews the alphabet
into signs of salt and scent
I regain a country
imagined from cellar to attic
where I come back to life stitch by stitch
in the lining of poppies
my memories as reredos

Ithaca Ithaca
sings the weaving hour
at last saved are my hieroglyphs
O macramé of sap
The rapid notes of the thrush
neither muezzins nor watchers
but portent of festivals

Oh annexed Father
son of my solitary works
fall is beautiful it is the season of October

DRAMA

RODERICK WALCOTT

CUL-DE-SAC

a play (excerpts)

AUTHOR'S NOTE
This play has remained faithful to the records of the battle in Saint Lucia between the British forces and the Republican Army of France. The work is written with a concern for its three languages: English, French, and French Creole. Translations are provided in the text to allow for a freedom of choice. Where no translation occurs, proper miming should prove sufficient between actor and audience. Thanks are expressed to Gregor Williams and to the Archaeological and Historical Society of St. Lucia; thanks also to Monique Angers for the French translations.

R.W.

For *McDONALD DIXON*

THE CHARACTERS
A WOMAN
A BRITISH CAPTAIN
A FRENCH LIEUTENANT

THE TIME
1796 — The 24th of May

THE PLACE
Morne Fortune, Saint Lucia, The West Indies

SCENE

Before the lights the sounds of battle, then quiet.
In the fading smoke an abandoned redoubt is visible.
On this small defence post with its grassy slope rests a cannon, with the back of another facing upstage. A half-moon shaped wall is in a state of disrepair.
Providing the frontal approach to this battery is a flight of steps, partially hidden by tall grass and stalks of sugar-cane.
More canes sprout like knotted spears beyond the walls of this little rampart, and in the distance a waving tri-colour, the Republican flag of France, can be seen.

(A woman enters dressed in soiled peasant clothes. She carries a large round basket on her head and two military belts across her breasts, supporting a second load on her back. In her hands are a hooked stick and cutlass for clearing bush. A sheath for the cutlass hangs from her waist. Under extreme physical stress and in a crouched position, she unloads the basket. After a great sigh, she kisses the ground.)

THE WOMAN
At last.   Ah.
(She crosses herself but stops half way.)
The beginning of the end.   Le commencement de la fin.
(She wipes herself, chuckling.)
But people load never too   May pachay pas jamais lou
heavy for theirself.   pour met-yo.

141

(She extracts a coconut from her basket and trims it with great skill. For her thoughts her recorded voice is heard.)

(The rest continues according to manuscript you have.)

(She splits the nut with one stroke of the cutlass and begins eating the kernel. As she eats she feels the ground with bare feet.)

THE WOMAN'S VOICE

The ground hard.	Terre-a raide.
The grass will be good	Zel-la kai bon

(Removes a flambeau from her basket.)

for the cane fire.	pour can-bwillay-a.

(Nervously) Last night I feel rain
sprinkle my face.

Woy, please — don't make it fall	Woy, pas faire-il tombay avan mwen fin twavail?

(Begins a quick crossing of herself only to stop again, then turns sharply to upstage let.)
before I finish?

(She lights the torch then signals feverishly, crouching towards upstage left. She waits. Very distant drumming makes her elated.)

THE WOMAN

A la fin! *(With muted shout.)*

Freedom will light our road!	La Liberté!

(She quickly extinguishes the torch at the sound of musket fire.)

Next time this lighting so bright even hell will veglay!	L'autre fois mwen limer sa, toute l'enfer kai veglay!

(Fans herself, sits.)
Bon.

(Sounds of a man's voice in her thoughts.)

A MAN'S VOICE

Let the white cocks fight their fight.	Quittay say cock blan-a tiway pwens.
If the French win we'll take Pavillon — but if the English beat them, is Martinique pour toute voltijay!	Si Fwancais-a gehyen, nous kai pwende-il la main yo — mais si l'Angleterre pwende Pavillon, say Martinique pour toute voltijay!

(With hand over brow she scans directly downstage.)

THE WOMAN'S VOICE

Ah yesterday that was fight. I believe have some English already on this hill. (Rises) But I must	Ah, sa tais bataille year. Mwen cwoeur ni un commesse Anglais ja moutay Morna-la,

142

start. If you wait for friend coal-pot you bound to die hungry.

oui. Tem Mwen commensay. Si ou espayway a sou canawie belle mer-ou, ou kai mor fain.

(Sound of a baby crying. She approaches the bag.)

THE WOMAN

Ah, you hungry, dou-dou?
(Kissing bundle.)
I was letting you sleep.
(She lifts bundle out of bag.)
Come meet mamma.

Ah, ou fain, por piti?

Mwen tais ka quittay-ou dormi.

Vin joeun mamma.

(She holds the bundle to her, and swaying slowly, begins a lullaby. She turns and begins to breast-feed the child. As she hums, her voice is heard again on tape.)

THE WOMAN'S VOICE

Two days leave ajoupa, climbing Barre de l'Isle, beat Chemin Royal and Bara-Bara to reach Derrière Fort for you, *(Kisses child.)* ti shou-shou.

Deux jour ka marchay pour-ou, dou-dou, hauteur Barre de l'Isle, quittay ajoupa en gwand bois, batte Chemin Royal, Bara-Bara, wivay Derrière Fort pour ou, ti shou-shou.

(A satisfied gurgle from the bundle as the woman ends the feeding. Battle sounds. The woman shivers, holding bundle closely.)

THE WOMAN'S VOICE

Ah, la ger terrible, but nothing worse than that sickness call slavery.

Ah la ger terrible, mais jamais comme maladie l'enslave.

(Sounds of man's voice again makes her pensive.)

THE MAN'S VOICE

Worse than every itch, chiga, fever or hurricane. Worse than any ending of the world.
(She lifts bundle endearingly.)

Sa-a mauvais passay toute peste, chiga, cyclon — passay toute l'enfer de moune.

THE WOMAN'S VOICE

All the others I lose — but you, dou-dou cher, will know what they call "liberté" for the rest of your life.
(Sways with bundle.)
Yes, is with patience you seeing red ant belly.

Tous les autres mwen ped — mais ou, dou-dou cher, ou kai connaitre sa yo ka cwier "la liberté" pour toute la vie-ou.

Ay oui, ec patience ou ka ouer bouden formi woute.

(Louder battle sounds.)

THE WOMAN

Good. Time for your hiding-place, chérie. I have my work to do.	Bon. Temps pour sayway-ou. Mwen ni twavaille mwen pour faire.

(She takes a cavassa cake from the basket and munches on it. She restraps the baby to her back, carefully lifts the basket to her head and hurriedly exists down the steps.

Sound of musketry, shouting and distant cannon.

A British Captain enters.

His trembling gait, vacant stare and jaundiced pallor shows an unhealthy condition. He collapses below the downstage cannon.

As he begins to speak, he appears to be addressing someone.)

THE BRITISH CAPTAIN

Orderly . . . *(Returns "salute")* . . . take a letter.
(His thoughts, through his recorded voice, are now heard.)

THE CAPTAIN'S VOICE

"Morne Fortunée. Twenty-fourth May, seventeen ninety six. My dearest one,
As I contemplate this lull of battle after a month's campaign, I recall most vividly the circumstanmces which have brought me hither. It may well be that I shall bear full blame for narrating these events which certain regiments would have wished forgotten — but the truth must be disclosed. Whilst straying from my company — no, delete that —er— we've made much headway to the top of this commanding peak. (Using a spyglass.) Now as the men-of-war unfurl to windward, I still see your kerchief off Weymouth in that fair Channel breeze.
But if a paradox exists as beauty being commonplace, my sweet, it must be here in these Antilles."

THE CAPTAIN

It were as if no terror sizzles under these royal palms.

THE CAPTAIN'S VOICE

"The enemy calls this age the dawning of delight, and have re-named the town Felicity. It's like a tinted cheeseboard in this strong light of dawn."

THE CAPTAIN

Oh I'd give up my commission for a sketch-pad and some water colours now! *(Using glass again.)*

THE CAPTAIN'S VOICE

"A narrow promontory called La Vigie the Lookout curves along the batteries of Choc Bay.

Beyond the channel in blue mist lies Martinique, from whence I came on His Majesty's Ship called *Charon*, of all things. It was like a final crossing in Stygian darkness to gaze now on this timely spectacle.

And if that were not feast enough, my love, behind me *(Looks upstage left, with glass.)* another vale so wide, so deep as sunlight swarms the cane tops — to a grander estuary.

There's a joke in the ranks which says to disembark here you Lookout for the Shock of landing in The Trap — for that grand bay and valley are both called Cul-de-Sac."

THE CAPTAIN

And that's how trapped I feel, duty-bound to this green corner of the world. *(Coughing.)* But we must press on before the rains.

(The sound of a woman's voice pleases him.)

A WOMAN'S VOICE

It's spring now on the Downs. What larks to be at Brighton, Hastings and The Hove! The hounds are stretching sure enough —

THE BRITISH CAPTAIN

But I'd give up all to be among the microscopes at Cambridge.

THE CAPTAIN'S VOICE

"Had I the choice of campaigns, love, it certainly wouldn't be here. Certainly much closer to you perhaps in Europe chasing that former lieutenant of artillery — that Corsican whose name escapes me."

THE CAPTAIN

For what are we here but guardians of naval stations? It's clear to every thinking man all must depend on our superiority at sea.

THE CAPTAIN'S VOICE

"When will they realize small garrisons are useless here, and expense for larger ones unnecessary?

But who am I to advise, a mere Captain — not even of the navy, *(Coughs.)* prone to sea-sickness *(Attempts to vomit. fails.)* despite a 'blue-jacket' family?

(A pause, sounds of musket fire.)

Our major battle plan has three points of attack. *(Using glass.)* Disembarkation for the first and second fleets are from Anse-du-Cap and Choc *(Looking to downstage right.)* to the town's north.

The third fleet and its landing point, I think, will be our

pièce-de-résistance.

THE BRITISH CAPTAIN
To win this battle we must subdue the fortress completely.

THE CAPTAIN'S VOICE
"I've been fortunate, I believe, to be commanded by Brigadier
General Moore, fresh from Corsica, in the second column of
the Fifty-Seventh. *(Smiles.)*
Do you remember when I turned down that commission
with the Guards?"

THE BRITISH CAPTAIN
You know I'm not one for ceremony.

THE CAPTAIN'S VOICE
"I sought rather an adventurous regiment for the honour and
glory of my country."

(Distant cannon.)

"What a long, painful task it's been. I feel as weary as the rock
of Sisyphus.
Now all must hinge on the morale of these troops, and here
I have grave apprehensions. The Government's insane policies
and delays of Ordinance are all excuses for incompetence.
But these men aren't martyrs to patriotism. They know
they're victims of imbecility.
Our generals with few exceptions are mental sluggards
fortified with gout and flatulence. Rank here is rank indeed. A
growing callousness has become legion with officers of my
caste. They are simply masquerading in the guise of famous
regiments.

THE BRITISH CAPTAIN
(Chuckling dryly.) More akin to the muming with fife and drum
found in these parts at Christmastide.

THE CAPTAIN'S VOICE
As to the lower orders, corporal punishment seems ineffective.
It's good this terrain's so rugged it discourages desertion."

THE BRITISH CAPTAIN
And who can say how much of the enemy's mischievous doc-
trines have seeped into these ranks? *(Shuddering.)*

THE CAPTAIN'S VOICE
"There's an island sickness here, my love, which I —" no
Orderly, strike that out — "which makes one realize death
looms not only in a black shroud. It can approach as golden
as the sun itself. This jaundiced fever with the ague working its
will among us is more formidable than the most indomitable foe."

146

THE BRITISH CAPTAIN
If we didn't need their crops, I'd say good riddance and hand these pestilential places back to France.

THE CAPTAIN'S VOICE
"It sets one wondering whether these investments of the Crown are more essential than the lives of a few thousand British soldiers.

Yet I pray God guide our flintlocks, for morale is at such a low ebb that it must get better. After all aren't we camped on a place called Lucky Hill, under a brigadier named Hope?"

(He tries again to vomit, fails and collapses. Battle sounds. A sudden explosion as a soldier is flung onstage by its force.

It is a French lieutenant who has sustained a shrapnel wound in his right leg. He remains in a temporary state of shock.

As he recovers he puts his three-cornered hat on then sees the British Captain, who has stirred from the blast.

The French Lieutenant draws his sword and limps cautiously towards the Captain. On a closer look, as the Captain awakens, he backs away, still poised. He throws his hat to the ground in amazement.)

THE FRENCH LIEUTENANT
Sacré bleu! La fièvre jaune d'ici!

(The Captain feebly tries aiming his pistol at the French Lieutenant. The other steps aside and knocks it out of the Captain's hand with the flat of his sword. The Lieutenant holds his leg in sudden pain but sits away from the Captain.)

Un capitain eh? Quel est votre nom?

A captain, eh? What's your name?

THE BRITISH CAPTAIN
Fifty-Seventh Light Regiment of Foot —

THE FRENCH LIEUTENANT
(Nodding.) Un chasseur à pied. Et votre nom?

Hmm. Light Infantry. And your name?

THE BRITISH CAPTAIN
First Brigade.

(The Lieutenant chuckles.)

THE FRENCH LIEUTENANT
Votre nom est un nombre, alors. *(Shrugs.)* Ce n'est rien, parce que vous allez mourir bientôt *(Chuckles.)* avec la

Your name is a number, then. That's nothing, because you'll die soon with the fever. I'm a Lieutenant of the Artillery.

147

fièvre. *(Indicating self.)* Je suis
un lieutenant d'artillerie.

THE BRITISH CAPTAIN
Vous allez mourir aussi avec la
blessure en votre jambe.

We'll see who dies first with
that wound in your leg.

THE FRENCH LIEUTENANT
So you understand Français.
(The Captain turns away.)
Un peu? *(No response.)*
En tout cas if I die with the leg
you die plus lentement — ah,
more slow, with le maladie
jaune?

THE BRITISH CAPTAIN
Tous les autres mouriront avec
vous dans la forteresse.

All will die with you in that
fortress.

THE FRENCH LIEUTENANT
(Shrugs.) Peut-être. But too
much is at stake here to have
time for dying. *(Pauses.)* What
you do, avant la guerre?

THE BRITISH CAPTAIN
Étudient. Natural science.
Université.

THE FRENCH LIEUTENANT
(Indicating self.) A farmer. From Aubigny — in the Loire valley.
When this is fini I do law and politique — at the Sorbonne.

THE BRITISH CAPTAIN
Mmmm. *(Almost to himself.)* The Age of Enlightenment *is* here
indeed.

THE FRENCH LIEUTENANT
Quoi?

*(The British Captain waves it aside. The Lieutenant, half rising,
looks downstage and continues.)*

Quel spectacle . . . un crayon, a few brush strokes — parfait.

THE BRITISH CAPTAIN
Vous-êtes a-a painter?

THE FRENCH LIEUTENANT
Must it be only for the landed gentry? *(Almost to himself.)* Ah,
oui, a scene worthy of our grand design.

148

You will lose mon capitaine, because your cause n'est pas juste. *(Pauses.)*

The very first explosion was necessaire you know, for the birth of paradise. So it is with this nouveau monde.

THE BRITISH CAPTAIN

Yes . . . the Creator at his Lookout send shock waves of war to our small Cul-de-Sac.

THE FRENCH LIEUTENANT

Oh, *(Chuckling.)* you know the joke among the ranks. *(Shaking his head.)* Ah toujours — le cynicisme d'Anglaise.

THE BRITISH CAPTAIN

For my part, you can have the bloody lot. But we must stop you spreading seditious seedlings in this garden — no matter how pestilential it is. That right's ours for being here first.

THE FRENCH LIEUTENANT

And what you do? Le chien   The dog in the manger.
dans la crêche.

You plant no roots, reap crops, leave weeds to foster this rebellion. Non, we own that right by staying. *(Pauses.)* I could be chasing Austrians now in Italy with Bonaparte.

THE BRITISH CAPTAIN

Ah, the name escapes me —

THE FRENCH LIEUTENANT

(Nodding.) Was a lieutenant of artillery, you know — comme moi.

Yes, but the rights of Man
call for action anywhere in this
world — not in Europe only.
(The Captain coughs.) In another
time, pour moi, with a few
livres colonial, a woman the
colour of good earth *(Turns to
upstage left.)* and a piece of that
valley — *(Forcefully.)* Il faut   We must cultivate our
cultiver notre jardins.   gardens!

THE BRITISH CAPTAIN

Votre paradis vert, *(Chuckling.)* dans les maladies tropiques. *(Battle sounds.)* Wake up from your utopia lieutenant. *(Using glass towards downstage right.)* Your seaward batteries at Labrelotte and Trouillac are abandoned. We've secured the south hills facing your garrison. How's that for instant shock?

THE FRENCH LIEUTENANT
Viens. I invite you to breakfast — on howitzers and cannon, with the best gunners in all Europe.

THE BRITISH CAPTAIN
Not any more.

THE FRENCH LIEUTENANT
Look capitaine, this is not just another war. Not eighteen years ago with Barrington and D'Estaing. It is the first awakening for a cause universel. The sun must rise on all men with the same intensity.

THE BRITISH CAPTAIN
Mmmm. A new sun for Charlotteville —

THE FRENCH LIEUTENANT
Non. Felicité. The dawning of Felicity Town in St. Lucie la Fidèle.

THE BRITISH CAPTAIN
Fecility indeed — with your hopes lying at anchor in a pestiferous temple teeming with treachery.

THE FRENCH LIEUTENANT
Betise. Our citoyens put self behind to hold on to the freedom we've provided. They're all citizen soldiers now.

THE BRITISH CAPTAIN
Not *soldier* citizens? *(Chuckles.)* I saw that from your retreat. Take your head out of the clouds, lieutenant. *(Pointing upstage left.)* We've bivouacked at Duchazeau. A thousand yards from your impregnable fort and breathing down your gaping gullet — how's that for a pretty pickle?

THE FRENCH LIEUTENANT
Take it then. I defy you. Our cause is impregnable. Soon you'll see who's besieged. *(A pause.)* Your assault yesterday showed the poor quality of your command.

THE BRITISH CAPTAIN
Oh?

THE FRENCH LIEUTENANT
If both columns had attached — ah — simulanté —

THE BRITISH CAPTAIN
Simultaneously —

THE FRENCH LIEUTENANT
You wouldn't have lost a dozen men. But your brigadiers seem more interested in personal glory —

THE BRITISH CAPTAIN
That Moore . . . much — much too impetuous . . .

THE FRENCH LIEUTENANT
Le superflu est très necessaire, you know. Where's the room for initiative in a simultaneous volley?

(The British captain swears under his breath. The lieutenant looks downstage slowly, to the left, and continues.)

Part of your fleet is heading south. *(Looking further left.)* To the grand bay?

(No answer. The French Lieutenant chuckles.)

I see they've avoided the warm welcome from Place-des-Armes.

THE BRITISH CAPTAIN
How little you see. We don't have to engage the town. We'll bombard it once we take Fort Charlotte.

THE FRENCH LIEUTENANT
Ah bien. Mais le plus difficile est toujours le dernier (to hold le fleche.

THE BRITISH CAPTAIN
(More to himself.) In my view *(with glass)* the best gradient for uphill assault *(Doing a slow, complete turn to upstage left)* would be from Camp Ferrands.

THE FRENCH LIEUTENANT
Well, our casualties measure the same. The battle's evenly poised, so rest in the calm of the fighting.

* * *

During this moment of tenuous calm, a verbal battle ensues.
The British Captain blasts the lieutenant's logic in his support of mass conscription for a people's army, while justifying army muskets being turned against a mob in the name of military discipline. In his broadside against the leaders of the French Republic, the captain ridicules their exploitation of the poor by bloodbaths and power politics. This is a necessary rite of purification, the Lieutenant counters, since the new morality of the revolution will replace the religion of its citizens.
The process of change and how it affects the human condition is advanced by the Captain to propound the thought of power corrupting. In his counter-thrust the Lieutenant insists the poor will remain the deciding force towards the acquisition of a perfect state. He further mocks the Captain's theory of an existing power which supersedes man's limitations. The Lieutenant presents a scientific denial

*of religious miracles, which will all be explained by the enlighten-
ment of man. In their conflicting views of morality and government,
both admit they are at an impasse.*
   The Lieutenant looks out to Cul-de-Sac Bay.

THE FRENCH LIEUTENANT
   Your third fleet should be in the bay by now. Where in the
   devil they?

The Captain smiles. A pause. The woman re-enters.
   *She is without the bundle at her back, but still carries the basket
on her head. With upright stance she appears surprised, as if
expecting the redoubt to be unoccupied. She stands firm, breathing
a sigh of resignation.)*

THE WOMAN
   (To the Lieutenant.) Bon jour. *(He nods and smiles.)*
   (To the Captain.) Morning. *(The Captain does not reply, but begins
   to chuckle.)*

THE BRITISH CAPTAIN
   (Clearing throat.) Your third estate, lieutenant?

THE FRENCH LIEUTENANT
   (Nodding, smiling.) Yes, with a few livres colonial . . .

THE BRITISH CAPTAIN
   Mmmm.

THE FRENCH LIEUTENANT
   The colour of good earth . . .

*(The Captain grunts, chuckles and coughs. The woman starts
unloading herself.)*

THE BRITISH CAPTAIN
   Never underestimate the power of an unknown force, Lieutenant. Such wild beauty can have its landslips — in deep valleys
   with tropical diseases.

(The woman stares at the Captain with a furious eye.)

THE WOMAN
   Nous toujours ka parlay moune mal, a force nous hayir cor
   nous.

THE BRITISH CAPTAIN
   What was that?

THE FRENCH LIEUTENANT
   She says we're always giving others the contempt we deserve.

THE BRITISH CAPTAIN
   Mmmm. Quite apepper tree, isn't she?

(The woman sits, fanning herself.)

THE WOMAN
   Ah, say temps terrible, sa.   Is bad time, eh?
   (Looks out slowly to left.)
   Say man-o-war-a ja passay   The man-o-war pass Marigot
   Marigot. pouchi yo pas   already. Why they don't stop at
   daybachay Cul-de-Sac?   Cul-de-Sac?

*(The Lieutenant shrugs, smiling. The woman keeps fanning, and
continues.)*

Mi matin chaud. Pani assay van. *(Looking up.)* Soleil ja haut.
Sembe kai ni plus mauvais temps.

THE FRENCH LIEUTENANT
   (Answering the Captain's quizzical look.) Just the weather, Captain.

*(The woman removes a coconut from her basket, starts trimming it.
The soldiers watch each other, amazed at her skill. She offers the
coconut to the Frenchman. He hesitates. She pours some on her
hand, tastes it to show it is good. He shrugs, smiles and accepts. She
cuts another, offering it to the British Captain. He turns away shiv-
ering.)*

THE WOMAN
   (To the Lieutenant.) Sa ki wivay-i? *(The Captain turns back.)*

THE BRITISH CAPTAIN
   Tell her we don't speak her gibberish.

*(The Lieutenant, drinking the coconut, has no time to answer as the
woman slowly approaches the Captain.)*

THE WOMAN
   La fievre jaune, eh?
   Mwen tais ni-i leur mwens tais   I have it when I was small.
   piti.

*(She returns to her basket, unwraps a small earthenware jug, well
corked, from it. She hands it to the British Captain, who begins to
move away. She goes and places his head on her lap. He resists
with all the strength possible.)*

You must take it. Si ou pas vlay more.

THE BRITISH CAPTAIN
   Get off with that jumbie juice, you jungle sorceressi.

THE WOMAN
Sa i di?

THE FRENCH LIEUTENANT
Il vous appele — la sorcière?

THE WOMAN
La ----- *(She bursts out laughing.)* ---- La sorcière?

(She laughs louder. She looks at the jug then at the Captain, and pockets the jug. Suddenly she rises angrily and stands over the British Captain, legs wide, hands on hips. She places her feet on his arms.)

THE BRITISH CAPTAIN
What're you — get off, you sleazy black —

(The woman pulls out his sword and pistol, flings them downstage. The Captain trembles, seething with fury. The woman watches the French Lieutenant, who stares at her, smiling. As she unsheathes her cutlass he keeps staring and smiling, but does not move. He sighs with relief as she cuts another coconut for herself. She looks back at the British Captain, chuckling.)

THE WOMAN
La sorcière noire. *(Laughs with the Lieutenant.)*

* * *

The woman is amiably questioned by the French Lieutenant. He learns she is carrying provisions for his garrison. The British Captain, however, believes she is a rebel spy for the "brigands" or escaped slaves. This was why she confiscated his weapons, he says. The Lieutenant explains she did not want to be caught in their crossfire, especially since the Captain refused her offer of medicine.

The Lieutenant, anxious for an ally, hears that the woman's common-law husband is an ex-slave fighting on the French side. He warns that they must win this battle or she will lose the freedom granted her by the revolution. The Lieutenant receives an uncertain response.

The woman suddenly sees the British army advancing behind Cul-de-Sac valley. The Lieutenant cannot understand why the battleships of the third fleet are not in the grand bay. The Captain laughs. He discloses the battle's pièce-de-résistance — the fleet has landed farther south, at Anse-La-Raye, to make their rear guard assault more penetrative. The woman, a rebel lookout, is fearful for her men below who are hiding behind the bay, since the advancing forces could surprise them in their hideout.

The battle for the southern slope begins as the three watch from the abandoned redoubt. After several inefficient attacks the British withdraw because, as the French Lieutenant observes, their assault lacked coordination.

Continuing to woo the woman to his cause, the Lieutenant compliments her as a most extraordinary person with her displays of wit, individuality and common sense. The Captain grudgingly admits she is. The woman tells them there are more like her, however, helping the cause of freedom in their own simple way. As the Lieutenant pleads his case, the woman appears more confused. She hates slavery with all her soul, but is uncertain of her path to freedom. The British soldier and the woman keep a guarded distance between them.

When asked her name the woman replies it is best they do not know each other, since it is only by a strange twist of fate they have met together, but might never meet again. The woman pulls out the rum and shares it with the Lieutenant. She regards the Captain with some concern.

THE WOMAN
I wish you try the medicine. What you have to lose?

THE BRITISH CAPTAIN
I - I'll have the drink i - instead . . .

(He groans, collapses. The woman goes quickly to the Captain. She props him against herself, dampens his mouth with the liquor. She then skilfully pours the medicine from her pocket into his mouth, which he takes then completely collapses.)

THE FRENCH LIEUTENANT
Why you comfort him? He is the enemy.

THE WOMAN
If he is to die, let's make his last hours pleasing.

(A pause, as the woman rocks the British Captain.)

THE FRENCH LIEUTENANT
I say all men are brothers, and you make it true with an unselfish action. *(Indicating the Captain.)* Peut-etre one he'll find out, if not too late.

THE WOMAN
Perhaps his brothers will.

(She rests the Captain down quietly.)

THE FRENCH LIEUTENANT
Perhaps all men.

THE WOMAN
L'enslave aussi?

THE FRENCH LIEUTENANT
L'enslave particularly.

THE WOMAN
And the sisters? I not so sure about the women.

THE FRENCH LIEUTENANT
Well, if I can't be your brother, perhaps — your lover, then?

THE WOMAN
Encore plus mal. Even less equal there. That's even worse.

THE BRITISH CAPTAIN
Bravo sorceress. *(Clapping.)* Well put.

(Both are stunned at his awakening.)

THE WOMAN
(With muted fury to both.) Yes, I'm the child-maker for all kind of men — perhaps with as many children — but definitely no lovers.

THE BRITISH CAPTAIN
St. Lucie la Fidèle. *(Chuckling.) Remember the inlets and the gorges, Lieutenant, and how many can hide there.*

THE FRENCH LIEUTENANT
Captain, if you can't say something pleasant, why not be still?

THE WOMAN
Oui, making children to fight both side, killing one another. (Then almost to herself.) We lift their weight on our head and reap their bones from out this dirt.

THE BRITISH CAPTAIN
(Giggling.) Touché, Lieutenant.

THE WOMAN
You too. *(Now the Lieutenant giggles.)* Children both side, Anglais today, French tomorrow . . . here today . . . *(A good pause.)* . . . tomorrow like sand in the wind.

THE FRENCH LIEUTENANT
How many children — en tout?

THE WOMAN
I - I don't know. From the time I change from child to woman. Some live, some die of sickness. All is gone — *(Then more a soliloquy, embracing herself.)* — except . . .

THE FRENCH LIEUTENANT
Quoi?

THE WOMAN
(Smiles, shakes head, shrugging with a weak laugh.(Was my night work — *(To Lieutenant.)* travaille la nuit — for the estate.

THE BRITISH CAPTAIN
(More to himself.) The deterioration of the times, perhaps — from gold to the iron of industry —

THE FRENCH LIEUTENANT
More like gold crosses branded on blacks with iron chains.

THE WOMAN
(To the British Captain.) Gadez. Tout sevel say enslave qui ka sevi liday mal.

THE BRITISH CAPTAIN
(To Lieutenant.) And what's that bon mot?

THE FRENCH LIEUTENANT
She thinks all minds are enslaved that serve things evil.

THE BRITISH CAPTAIN
Mmmm . . . that pepper tree . . .

THE WOMAN
The iron of war is nothing comme l'usine enslave.

THE FRENCH LIEUTENANT
Je vous crois.
I believe you.
La fer chaud sur la cervelle.

(To the Captain.) Slavery, mon Capitaine — branding-irons on the brain —

THE WOMAN
Plus chaud *(Looking up.)* passay soleil sa-a. Nothing can burn like esclavage. I cannot run fast enough with the chains in my head even my feet is free.

THE BRITISH CAPTAIN
(To the Lieutenant.) Ah — *(The woman looks down at upstage left wall.)*

THE WOMAN
To escape the factory there for the iron up here, *(She runs to downstage cannon.)* grand fer *(She sticks her face near the cannon's mouth.)* — to tear off our heads — *(Takes her head away.)* but are our heads still there? *(Slowly sitting.)* Sometimes I wish they wasn't, from the weight of these times . . .

She takes up two cannon balls. Distant sound of guns, then native drums. The woman listens, then collects her thoughts. She knocks the cannon balls together a few times.)

. . . just to satisfy your bals de fer.

Louder drums. She places the balls against her ears, screaming.

Aieee . . . *(Battle sounds.)* . . . wars and engines . . . *(Looks from Lieutenant to Captain.)* . . . cannon — *(Stares at Briitish Captain.)* and factory — *(Stares at French Lieutenant.)* factory — *(Back at Captain.)* — and cannon.

With an anguished gasp she takes the cannon balls from her ears, holds them to her breast.

. . . crushing . . . crushing . . .

She places cannon balls at the base of the downstage cannon, and with a wild shout runs to the front of the gun. She stands astride it facing the men, back to the cannon, and undulates her pelvis in both terror and ecstasy, while looking in a haze to upstage left.)

. . . with the load of all men sur la terre.

THE BRITISH CAPTAIN
(Holding his own ears.) God, fill my ears with grapeshot! What savagery . . .

THE WOMAN
Yes, sauvage. *(She gets off cannon, takes cannon balls.)* Here, tin soldiers. Play with your toys.

She rolls a cannon ball to the Captain, then to the Lieutenant. She pauses.)

But while there is a soul in prison . . . a child to be born, no one — personne — is free.
    Alors, what is liberty? *(To the French Lieutenant.)* Liberté say twavaille qui pas ka fini.

THE BRITISH CAPTAIN
What *is* liberty, Lieutenant?

THE FRENCH LIEUTENANT
Unfinished business, mon capitaine.

THE WOMAN
Sa say liberté. Comme z'affaire toute femme. All we must do is owe our brothers all that is in our force to give, and leave the rest to . . .

THE FRENCH LIEUTENANT
No. Not to any mystic power. *(To the Captain.)* All her life she's been giving, expecting nothing in return. For the toil of her people we can never return we must pay her back by l'égalité de jouissance. Equality of benefits must be our ultimate . . .

158

THE BRITISH CAPTAIN
Your government's attempt to wipe out private property failed.

THE FRENCH LIEUTENANT
That doesn't follow it was wrong — or couldn't be tried again.
     You think the first and second estates should persist in their decay? With little to the most and the best for a chosen few?
     How does it go, Captain, in your holy book? Le dernier sera le premier?

THE BRITISH CAPTAIN
So you preach envy and wilful destruction of private property.

THE FRENCH LIEUTENANT
How can she respect what she's never owned?
     Our citizens' republic must have the right to confiscate or destroy property not vital to Man's natural needs — or the third estate will be picked clean by carrion crows joined as a corporate body.

THE BRITISH CAPTAIN
Aye, back to primeval states . . .

THE FRENCH LIEUTENANT
But first we level everything. Annihilate the past to understand the rights of ownership in this age. Until that happens property for me will always be another words for theft.

THE WOMAN
I cannot say for true I miss not to have property. I suppose I would feel better if I have. I should for those coming after me.
     Land in the old country had more valeur, they say — a place to rest after strife, and the spirit of your people staying there long after they was gone.
     So I was always close to the land, even I never have mine. My life you see was always measure by cane harvest.

| Piz zeb say la force en l'air, mais en bas nous toutes say verts terres. | Grass is the force on earth, you see, but below we're all earth-worms. |

THE FRENCH LIEUTENANT
After la guerre, you'll have the right to claim your husband's property as his compagne and bearer of his children.

THE WOMAN
M'a légitime . . .

THE FRENCH LIEUTENANT
Légitimate, pas légitime, c'est la même chose.

THE WOMAN
(Elated.) Vwai? Sa kai un bon True? That'll be a good law.
loi.

THE BRITISH CAPTAIN
Now you've got her so greedy she'll turn her noble savage to a
property-grabbing vixen.

THE FRENCH LIEUTENANT
You'll see how amusing it is when we confiscate your property.

THE BRITISH CAPTAIN
For whom? Your "sans culottes"? The rabble you'll teach a sense
of decency, who have no respect for their superiors or religious
precepts?

THE FRENCH LIEUTENANT
Show me the morality in your religious institutions, Captain,
especially with property. You think the clergy should remain
untaxed for centuries, preaching brotherly love while condoning
slavery? Using last rights and extreme unctions to grab property
through heavenly bribes for passages to paradise?

THE WOMAN
I hear at L'Abbaye, Terre Fournier was church land work by slave.

THE BRITISH CAPTAIN
The Pope has publicly denounced your revolution.

THE FRENCH LIEUTENANT
Well we excommunicate him from the society of rational men for
his ecclesiastical extreme. What about you? You resisted Papists in
your country.

THE BRITISH CAPTAIN
Yes, but not by desecrating sacred objects.

THE FRENCH LIEUTENANT
You should have been in Paris when we celebrated inside Notre
Dame.

THE WOMAN
Notre Dame cathedral? The Church of Our Lady, Mother of God?

THE FRENCH LIEUTENANT
Yes. We reconsecrated it —

THE BRITISH CAPTAIN
To the cult of reason and profaned the sepulchre of St. Denis.

THE WOMAN
T-That was what I couldn't take. At Dauphin, the broken statues of
St. Vièrge . . . in Louvet mother enviolay in their bed — and the
children . . . (She shivers) — but I suppose they bring it on themself.

THE BRITISH CAPTAIN
No. Don't makes excuses for such savagery.

THE FRENCH LIEUTENANT
A necessary ablution, mon capitaine. *(To the woman)* Remember chérie, there are no estates in heaven — only many mansions — and on earth the rights of kings are no longer divine.

THE BRITISH CAPTAIN
The people must be subject to a sovereign will.

THE FRENCH LIEUTENANT
Yes. *(Chuckling.)* "God save the King." We got tired of his fooling the assemblies . . .

THE BRITISH CAPTAIN
So you caught him at Varennes and killed him -- and with your muskets reversed . . .

THE FRENCH LIEUTENANT
Exterminated that vermin called the constitutional monarchy, and the ancien régime will never be the same.

THE BRITISH CAPTAIN
God help us all.

THE FRENCH LIEUTENANT
If the king is guilty, the citizens have every right to eject him. Governments must be ruled by men, not men as gods, for all men are divine. Nations reach out to their people. Why must subjects bow to a king?

THE BRITISH CAPTAIN
I have a right to fight for king and country . . .

THE FRENCH LIEUTENANT
Yes, "Dieu et Mon Droit," pas mon *roi*. Right for the land of your forefathers, not the king. And what kings? Mad George? Inconsequential Louis? *(Chuckling dryly.)* "L'état c'est moi." Jamais! L'état est toujours nous, the people! Toute le monde est l'état, tonnerre! Before everything — the king.
Who runs the nobles and the clergy? The king. Qui est le souverain absolu? *(The woman laughs.)*

THE WOMAN
The king.

THE FRENCH LIEUTENANT
The symbol of stupidity?

THE FRENCH LIEUTENANT AND THE WOMAN
The king. *(Both laugh wildly.)*

THE BRITISH CAPTAIN
   Sir . . .

THE FRENCH LIEUTENANT
   (Singing.) "Here's a health unto his majesté.,

THE FRENCH LIEUTENANT AND THE WOMAN
   "With a fa-la-la-la-la-la-la"
   (Laughter by both.)

THE FRENCH LIEUTENANT
   As for his wife, that Austrian whore . . .

THE BRITISH CAPTAIN
   Lieutenant!

THE FRENCH LIEUTENANT
   (With mock feminine imitation.) "Let them eat cake."
      "Qu'ils mangent de la brioche." A bon-bon pour les Bour-
   bons. *(Spits.)* Putaine royale.

THE BRITISH CAPTAIN
   Guard your tongue sir. If you've no consideration for others, at
   least respect their causes — for "while I disagree with everything you say . . ."

THE FRENCH LIEUTENANT
   "I'll defend to the death your right to say it." I should have
   known. All cynics have a taste for M'sieur Voltaire. But you
   must respect our passions, capitaine.

THE BRITISH CAPTAIN
   To control them, sir, is what makes us rule the animal kingdom.

THE WOMAN
   I not know about raison that is for you nommes philosof. But
   what I feel is passion is the strongest force of all — stronger
   than raison, more strong than spirit self. What you need is to
   find plaisir to fight pain. Is the wheel where all our feelings
   turn.

THE BRITISH CAPTAIN
   The sensuality of the primitive.

THE FRENCH LIEUTENANT
   We must learn not to fear our passions, but use them for a
   righteous cause. The beast will always be inside us. Passion
   gives us the energy to protest for justice and destroy evil manifestations. *(To the woman.)* Tell me, ma chère — when did your
   passion feel the Revolution?

*In reply to the Lieutenant, the woman says that her inspiration for
the revolution came when she heard how the women marched in
France. When the republic's leaders in St. Lucia announced the
abolition of slavery and equality for all citizens, the woman
confesses such a vision of liberty in her lifetime was beyond her
wildest dreams. She remembers celebrating the capital, but also her
former life as a slave. Rebelling against the tyranny of the estates
she joined the "can-buillay" forces to burn the canes, only to be
caught and severely punished. She shows the welts from whiplash
on her back.*

*The terrible fear of losing her freedom remains as she tells of mil-
itary units being disbanded, and the prospect of returning to slave
labour in the fields in time of peace. The Lieutenant assures her
that under the new republic freedom will persevere both in peace
and war. Nevertheless she mentions that she and her man had
thoughts of deserting with their baby to the mountains.*

*When she discloses that she fought with the French in the victory
at Rabot, a battle which helped to replace the tri-colour on the fortress where it now waves, the Lieutenant begins to admire her even
further.*

*The Lieutenant talsk of his own life as a farmer. He is particu-
larly incensed by the death of his father resisting royal taxation and
dying in debtors' prison. The woman and the Lieutenant feel even
closer to each other in discovering they are both poor country folk
engaged in a class struggle.*

*In a picnic atmosphere on the battlefield, the woman offers food
and drink in the noonday heat. The British Captain refuses. The
Lieutenant and the woman join in singing the "Marseillaise," and
in his wild enthusiasm the Lieutenant rises, but falls in a hail of
musket fire.*

*While treating the Lieutenant's wound, the woman extracts a bul-
let from his shoulder. Their closeness ends in a passionate kiss. The
British Captain mocks this with a song.*

*The sound of cannon makes the woman tear herself from the
Lieutenant's arms. Looking over the small rampart she sees the
British men-o-war of the third fleet enter Cul-de-Sac Bay. Her fears
are cooled by the Lieutenant, and she hurries to him. In a nervous
state, she says she must tell him something.*

THE FRENCH LIEUTENANT
Qu'est que-ce?

THE WOMAN
Just now? *(Pause.)* I - I lie. I not from Mabouya. I come from
Barre de L'Isle.

THE FRENCH LIEUTENANT
So?

THE WOMAN
   You see my man didn't stay in l'armée citoyen. We was hiding
   in the hills with our child.

   The Captain laughs. The woman indicates her basket.

   The provision is for our own soldats. *(Looking upstage left.)*
   Only we didn't know the man-of-war would come from Anse-
   La-Raye to stay Cul-de-Sac.

THE BRITISH CAPTAIN
   She thought the centre of operations would be from the Lookout . . .

THE FRENCH LIEUTENANT
   Yes . . . La Vigie . . .

THE BRITISH CAPTAIN
   Just like the Barrington in seventy-eight. *(Chuckles.)* Oh no,
   Lieutenant, *(Laughing.)* that was our master coup. *(Laughing
   again.)* Oh that Abercrombie, what a general! *(With spyglass.)*
   Now for some true bluejacket broadsides at your southern
   slopes. *(Chuckling.)* What was that again Lieutenant — a fight
   to the finish?

THE WOMAN
   (To the Lieutenant.) I - I have to set a fire — a canbuillay for
   our escape.
     I tell my man fighting with Citoyen Goyrand is good, but he
   laugh and say he was tired to be between two connonade.
   (Pauses.) I - I'm sorry.

THE FRENCH LIEUTENANT
   (To the woman.) Is there any way to warn them? Do you have
   signals for a change in plan?

THE WOMAN
   N - No!

   Distant battle sounds. The Captain looks upstage right.

THE BRITISH CAPTAIN
   They're setting up more batteries at Duchazeau. And there are
   our reinforcements. *(Chuckles)* Why I think it's the rest of our
   regim,ent. *(Looks closer.)* It is! This will help the commander
   make the investment of the fortress complete. *(Looks more to
   the right.)* These engineers are so bloody slow. We've got to get
   supplies to the invested lines.
THE FRENCH LIEUTENANT
   Why that's almost sixteen kilometres and divided by this hill.
   C'est impossible. Ah, mais excusez-moi. I forget your miracles.

164

Louder sound of cannon. The woman looks to downstage right, towards the audience.

THE WOMAN
The English attacking La Vigie!

THE FRENCH LIEUTENANT
They're being beaten back.

THE BRITISH CAPTAIN
The ignorance of those officers! *(Looks closer with glass.)* Never saw such terrible advancing. How little they've learnt from the American campaign.

Sound of muskets and cannon.

THE FRENCH LIEUTENANT
Another barrage. *(Chuckling.)* A great many are falling, Captain. . .

THE WOMAN
And the rest running back!

THE BRITISH CAPTAIN
Dammit! *(Turns to upstage right.)* Wait — they're constructing a second line of advanced batteries at Duchazeau.
    And by Jupiter I was right. They will conduct a siège at Camp Ferrands.

THE FRENCH LIEUTENANT
Your new offensive has as much holes as our lady's basket, *(Stressing the jibe.)* "general."

THE BRITISH CAPTAIN
There go the Grenadiers . . . they're advancing well . . .

THE FRENCH LIEUTENANT
With your brigadier . . .

THE BRITISH CAPTAIN
Yes, that's Moore . . . *(Sound of musket fire.)*

THE FRENCH LIEUTENANT
He's placed himself between the two companies . . .

THE BRITISH CAPTAIN
They're reaching the summit . . . *(More rifle fire.)*

THE FRENCH LIEUTENANT
But being repulsed. There's your commander looking quite — ah boulversé . . . perturbed.

THE BRITISH CAPTAIN
It seems his orders were not to attack the post. It would have

been better to effect a lodgement. *(Turns to the right.)* on the
other side till a covered communication could be made.

THE FRENCH LIEUTENANT
There. Your brigadier feels he must take it. He's giving orders...

THE BRITISH CAPTAIN
Oh that Moore . . .

THE FRENCH LIEUTENANT
And more again. That old self, that culd of Narcissus. But then
you people can't forget personal glory, can you?

Sounds of shouting, musketry and cannon.

THE BRITISH CAPTAIN
He - he's storming the post. Looks like he's getting there. Yes,
he's made the summit with few losses. That Moore's completely undisciplined — yet he's full of initiative, you know.
    By gad sir, that's spirit to the heroic flame!

THE FRENCH LIEUTENANT
Caught between fires, impulsive, disobeying orders — that's
cannon fodder, sir.

THE BRITISH CAPTAIN
(More to himself.) But I must compliment John Moore. Thought
he was just a cocky, glory-seeker brigadier, but he's got a foresight that bespeaks military genius.

THE FRENCH LIEUTENANT
Observed no doubt by one familiar with it?

*The woman suddenly unsheathes the French Lieutenant's sword
and stands for a moment with determination.*

THE WOMAN
I make up my mind. My man and me not fighting like those
soldats negres on both side in your wars. That's not for my
grandchildren.

THE FRENCH LIEUTENANT
So what happened to our agreement? A while ago it was "Vive
La République."

THE BRITISH CAPTAIN
Hmm. Has "The Dawn of Felicity" waned so soon? I told you
beware of the landscape's beauty, Lieutenant — and *it's* diseases. The "yellowjack's" nothing compared to the treachery of
those minds burning with cane fires.
    There's no conscience here. No passion save from the heart.

THE WOMAN

Pas toute bagai choeur-ou ka   Not everything the heart telling
di sevelle.   the mind.
   Conscience have its own seasoning.

THE FRENCH LIEUTENANT

What about brotherhood?
   The family of Man? The rights of the dispossessed and the
land of your forefathers?

THE WOMAN

I - I don't care about your brotherhood.
I - I care about mine.

THE FRENCH LIEUTENANT

You lie!

She stares at him for a long pause as the sword trembles in her
hand.

THE WOMAN

You two was fighting long before my fathers come.
Oui, fwères la mor, fwères   Yes, brothers of death, brothers
d'enfer.   of hell.
Today fight, tomorrow wine, whiskey, sign some paper. La ger
gentilhommes. And we cut cane till your next fight for more
honour, more glory preaching St. Pierre and St. Paul.

Sound of cannon. She points upstage left.

My man in a next of gunpowder there. Any time they can
dayfonsay him from the hill and sea. Is my duty to . . .

THE FRENCH LIEUTENANT

Chérie . . .

THE WOMAN

(Screaming.) Non!
   We tired being piece of nothing.
   We must grow our jardin to die here, for our body to pass it
spirit from this land to my fathers and bless my children —
and to hell with you and the rest of them!

THE BRITISH CAPTAIN

(Chuckling.) A country ruled by brigands and deserters?

THE FRENCH LIEUTENANT

You'll never get there alone. They'll enslave you again, make
soup with your bnrains — faire le potage avec votre sevelle.
   Please. Trust me — s'il vous plait. You cannot abandon our
cause.

THE WOMAN

What cause? *(The Captain chuckles.)* You can save them on the
beach down there? *(A pause.)* Save them now and I'll come
back to your cause. *(Pause.)* Can you save them? *(Pauses again.)*
Can you?

THE FRENCH LIEUTENANT

I - I'll be truthful and say I can't.

THE WOMAN

I thought so.

THE FRENCH LIEUTENANT

But that's part of the conditions your liberty must pay for.
Remember what I said about blood sacrifice?
    Your companions I'm sure didn't do this without consider-
ing they might die for their freedom. All that's part of the
price. . .

THE WOMAN

No!

THE FRENCH LIEUTENANT

Forget your comrades-in-arms. It is a necessary sacrifice.

THE WOMAN

Ec conscience mwen?

THE FRENCH LIEUTENANT

Conscience is in the mind, not the spirit ma chère. In time it'll
disappear. Your friends betrayed the cause just as you did me
twice.

THE WOMAN

Ah, St. Pierre . . .

THE FRENCH LIEUTENANT

But I forgive you. *(Pauses.)* Come. Let's put our minds together
and finish this battle for a lasting peace.

THE WOMAN

(Quietly.) Non. *(Holding sword by the blade, looking up at the hilt.)*
I have enough from La Crosse already, *(While Captain chuckles.)* as the English say. *(Puts sword away from the Lieutenant.)* I
must spark the flame to light my way to liberté.

*The woman goes to the basket, lights the torch. She begins
signalling to upstage left.*

THE FRENCH LIEUTENANT

(To the Captain.) Stop her from signalling! She's the lookout!

The woman dashes off with the lighted torch. The Captain, spyglass fixed on the battle below, chuckles dryly and tells the Lieutenant not to worry; she is too late.

The woman's torch catches the cane and dry grass, as rebel slaves from the beach begin setting fires, also. They are shot. Flames spread far and wide as the woman, below the hill, lights around the redoubt.

The battleships in Cul-de-Sac begin their broadsides. Through his spyglass the Captain sees rebel canoes being blasted out of the water as other slaves, turning and swimming back are shot from the hill.

The woman, fearful that her common-law husband might be killed, asks the Captain if he can see a blue and yellow canoe — but the smoke and afternoon glare make it impossible to discern anything. The woman becomes depressed. She believes her comrades-in-arms are all destroyed. The Captain accuses her of relinquishing her duty and deserting her people as she listened to the Frenchman's honeyed words on liberty and the republic. Conscience-stricken, she sees the Captain as St. Paul to her inquisition. She is now between him and "St. Peter" the French Lieutenant, to whom she lied.

The cry of a baby disturbs the proceedings. Both sildiers are completely perplexed as the woman returns with her child from its hiding place. She answers the Lieutenant that she refused to keep it in the garrison because she has lost too many already. This last one must be hers to mould.

While the woman breast-feeds the baby, the battle again stirs. General Moore, full of enthusiasm and initiative, has gained the other side of the hill. He directs the battle with flair and imagination. The rough terrain is a serious deterrent however, and his offensive is again repulsed. Moore's success in this battle now appears dubious. His career is apprently at stake. As defeat stares him in the face he pleads with his commander for a final offensive, despite severe losses. Finally he is granted that request and launches this last attack. Led by the 27th Inniskilling Fusiliers in a glorious charge, the battle now takes an amazing turn. The British, after following up their success with the bayonet, force a French retreat, and the garrison finally lays down its arms. Despite frantic shouts of war to the uttermost by the wounded Lieutenant, the British have indeed won. The Captain even though ailing hails this triumph and taunts the Lieutenant about the age of miracles. The Lieutenant weeps and beats the earth in total frustration.

The three on the hill hear the victorious commander praise the valour of the Inniskillings. The sound of thunder precipitates a shower for the hurricane season's first rains. The woman rants against the commander-in-chief for his lack of praise for black regiments killed on both sides. She foresees her own armageddon with both the oncoming wet season and a resurgence of slavery under British rule. The Frenchman scoffs at the concept of the ending of the world, and declares it against all laws of natural science. In the woman's rage against the Lieutenant, he accuses her of turning against him because he has lost. In turn she ridicules his disbelief in a supreme deity.

The victorious performance of the Inniskillings is further commended by the commanding general, as he promises that the name "St. Lucia" will be inscribed with other glorious achievements of the 27th on this memorable day at Morne Fortune. The Frenchman cynically recalls the name given by the revolution to the island — St. Lucie "La Fidèle."

The three in the redoubt listen as the commander-in-chief, in tribute to General Moore, refers to him as the major inspiration behind that victorious Inniskilling charge.

THE BRITISH CAPTAIN

"Hail Inniskillings, let thy fame Emblaze thy country's story; and every tongue confess thy name Synonymous with glory!"

As the music continues the French Lieutenant speaks, at first almost to himself.

THE FRENCH LIEUTENANT

The Revolution might seem to have waned, my Captain, but in this jardin we've tended our seedlings well. Whatever you weed out, the rest will spring up in their consciousness again.

THE WOMAN

(Indicating the Captain.) A-dans conscience-li too.

THE FRENCH LIEUTENANT

She says in your conscience as well.

The Captain chuckles dryly.

So while I don't have my brushes and mon peinture for this sunset, for me it wouldn't be the red of crimson lake — non, but a vermilion — a red with the passion for living, for righteous anger and can-bwillay.

THE WOMAN

D'accord.

THE FRENCH LIEUTENANT

You talk of divine guidance yet still haven't found your own self-revelation — to set aside your taste of darkness to uplift the same spirit as your fellow man. Yes, man's magniture in our Enlightenment is still uplifting even in defeat. We've rekindled a concern for the common man as part of the commonwealth, the public welfare.

We've provided a vision of all men climbing towards liberty, equality and true brotherhood.

Offstage music. Cheering rises.

So as you trumpet your victory, can you honestly say you've learned nothing here today?

THE BRITISH CAPTAIN
(Uneasily.) Be quiet, man.

The French Lieutenant and the woman freeze in changing light. The Captain's voice is heard through atape recording.

OTHER VOICE
General Abercrombie sir, soldiers of His Majesty's Army in the Caribbees.

I most humbly thank our commander for the honours conferred this day upon me and the Regiment of the 27th Inniskillings. I take up this new post with the same zeal and sense of duty which I have tried to display throughout my career as a soldier for my king and country. After so hazardous an engagement not only with an ancient enemy but its government of new ideas, the iron will of discipline is necessary to rebuild this country and settle for a lasting peace. *(Distant applause.)*

As to the third forces on this island, those who have continued their personal and private war against both our armies — *(Drums roll.)* — a proclamation of free pardon to all who'd come within our lines and deliver up their arms —

THE WOMAN
(Shouting.) Dépandan we never crawl in labou esclavage again.

THE BRITISH CAPTAIN
No conditions! Only conditional surrender for brigands and deserters!

OTHER VOICE
My first order for this administration is that all crops will be requisitioned.

We appreciate the position of those Royalist planters and the bitterness sown between them and their slaves, after their supposed abolition under the past government.

THE FRENCH LIEUTENANT
(Angrily.) Quoi? "Supposed" abolition?

OTHER VOICE
We shall always ensure there are no reprisals for these maroons and runaways, as well as for those fighting in the reg-

iments of both countries.

To the planters under our new military order, let me say put out the fires of fear and hatred that rage even now. Plant new crops in this fertile garden not with swords but ploughshares. *(A distant rumbling.)*

As to those who have listened to that mischievous gospel of freedom, they must face the reality of returning to their masters to plough the soil now lying fallow, in order to stave off the dark clouds of starvation threatening this land. This we promise we shall enforce and return all able-bodied men and women, bondmen as well as free black to the estates under British rule. *(Drum rolls.)* This I swear by the sword of Saint George and His Royal Majesty King George the Third of England!

"God save the King" shouted in chorus offstage as the British National Anthem is played and the union jack rises slowly upstage. The woman lets out a deep cry.

THE WOMAN
No. Tell me is not what I hear. Back to the whip and the fields, cane crushing our bones and blood? The sugar and molassie not bitter then, O God?

I have nothing to cool my passion now. Let all disaster fall on me! Boots, blood and mud on my small hill of grass — cannonade my belly, carambolage my womb! Aie — aie — aie!

OFFSTAGE VOICE
Silence that woman!

Sounds of shouting offstage. Lieutenant points downstage right.

THE FRENCH LIEUTENANT
Félicitéville's burning!

THE BRITISH CAPTAIN
Aye — fire from the artillery and Place-des-Armes. But you mean Charlotteville certainly —

THE WOMAN
Carénage, Charlotteville, Castries — what's a name? The town still on fire!

Ay ben, sa say au fond bawie pour mwen.	Well done, is bottom of the barrel for me.

After that strong taste of freedom I must be slave again? Jamais! *(Loud then soft.)* Never, never, never, never.

The baby cries.

THE BRITISH CAPTAIN
Careful with the child —

THE WOMAN
So what I must do now? *(Looks at the child.)* Tells it there have
no freedom? No whips and scorns and tears? Better I fling it
(Lifting child high.) in this fire —

THE CAPTAIN AND THE LIEUTENANT
No!

THE WOMAN
Than live in ignorance and misery again.

THE FRENCH LIEUTENANT
Please — our cause is eternal no matter who wins or loses.

THE WOMAN
You had nothing to lose but honour and glory, but we —

Putting child down, crying and praying.

God I believe you up there — so please hear me now! Inter-
cede for us O mother of mothers. Sancta Maria, ora pro nobis,
help us in the hour of our —

THE FRENCH LIEUTENANT
(Shouting at the woman.) Get up from there with that désordre
comme une femme folle!

THE WOMAN
You calling me mad? Sir, respect yourself!

THE FRENCH LIEUTENANT
I say get up from there with that superstitious bétise — *(Chuckling.)* Sorcière noire —

*The woman lets out a guttural cry, unsheathing the cutlass, as the
Lieutenant tries to rise with his good arm, she slashes him in the
groin. The Captain quickly crawls to a sword and lunges at the
woman as she turns towards him. She grips her side and turns back
to the Lieutenant, who is groaning deeply.*

THE FRENCH LIEUTENANT
Y - You didn't understand — couldn't control your passion . . .
Notre raison est toujours juste . . . it cannot fail even you kill
us over and over again . . .

*The Lieutenant collapses. The woman holds the Lieutenant close to
her, quietly weeping as she closes his eyes.*

THE WOMAN
L - Look at the mess . . . grass, dirt and blood on bright colour
uniforms . . .

*Resting the Lieutenant gently down, sahe moves without a weapon
towards the British Captain, who is poised with his sword.*

THE BRITISH CAPTAIN

Not a step closer or you'll get more of the same. The fever's gone and I'm not too sick to defend myself/

THE WOMAN

(Nodding, but in a haze.) I'm glad the fever gone . . . *(Looking down at her wound and smiling.)* Is nothing. What's another mark on my body?

THE BRITISH CAPTAIN

Hope it festers in your womb for the next thousand generations.

THE WOMAN

(Chuckling dryly.) Ah, who have the passion now?

Sound of deep rumbing again.

O, God, the rain. *(The baby cries. She picks it up.)* But I don't need any of you to get my freedom. I'll find the force myself no matter how long — *(To baby.)* Come chérie. Back to the hills. We have business to fini.

THE BRITISH CAPTAIN

Are you daft, lady? You couldn't penetrate these lines — and even if you did there's smoke from the rain. If you're thinking of the sea, there aren't any more boats, and the men-of-war are still looming out there. Why not even a miracle —

THE WOMAN

I not afraid to die. *(Picks up cutlass.)* I already see the ending of the world.

THE BRITISH CAPTAIN

But the baby —

THE WOMAN

If we stay, better we dead.

She waves cutlass for a goodbye, moves sharply off.

OFFSTAGE VOICE

Stop that woman!

The woman freezes in her tracks for a moment.

THE BRITISH CAPTAIN

(Looking towards the voice then the woman.) No, no!

The woman starts dashing off again. Offstage shooting. Sound of barrage of gunfire from upstage.

THE BRITISH CAPTAIN

(Shouting towards barrage.) You stupid fools!

The woman stops again. The Captain is frozen in disbelief. The sound of rain. The woman drops to her knees with the child. She crawls groaning in front of the Captain, and falls protecting the baby. The Captain, almost weeping, picks it up.

OFFSTAGE VOICE
Bring me that child!

To the sound of rolling kettle drums, the British Captain slowly extends his arms with the child in the act of presenting.

The drums suddenly stop.
COMPLETE BLACKOUT.

Then martial music, "I Vow To Thee My Country" for the ending of the play.

MOSAIC PRESS FICTION SERIES
Quality fiction at reasonable prices

Fool *by Leon Whiteson*
The Gates by Marion Andre Czerniecki
A Long Way to Oregon *by Anne Marriott*
A Strange Attachment and Other Stories
 by Bibhutibhusan Bandyopadhy, translated
 from the Bengali by Phyllis Granoff
Cracked Wheat and Other Stories *by Hugh Cook*
A Dialogue with Masks *by Mary Melfi*
The Far Side of the River: Selected Short Stories
 by Jacob Zipper, translated
 from the Yiddish by M. Butovsky
Big Bird in the Bush: Stories and Sketches
 by Earle Birney
The Honey Drum: Seven Tales from Arab Lands
 by Gwendolyn MacEwen
Summer at Lonely Beach and Other Stories
 by Miriam Waddington
The Suicide *by Nikolai Erdman, translated*
 from the Russian by A. Richardson & Eileen Thalenb
Cogwheels and Other Stories *by Akutagawa Ryunosuke,*
 translated from the Japanese by E. Norman
Vibrations in Time *by David Watmough*
A Long Night of Death *by Alberto Balcarze*
Not Enough Women *by Ken Ledbetter*
Tass is Authorized to Announce *by Julian Semyonov*
Cold Blood: Murder in Canada *ed. by Peter Sellers*
The Year of Fears *by David Watmough*
A Shapely Fire: Changing the Literary Landscape
 ed. by Cyril Dabydeen